THE JOY OF RETIREMENT

Summersdale Publishers Ltd
46 West Street
Chichester
West Sussex
PO19 1RP
UK

www.summersdale.com

Printed and bound in the Czech Republic

ISBN: 978-1-84953-661-5

Substantial discounts on bulk quantities of Summersdale books are available to corporations, professional associations and other organisations. For details contact Nicky Douglas by telephone: +44 (0) 1243 756902, fax: +44 (0) 1243 786300 or email: nicky@summersdale.com.

THE JOY OF RETIREMENT

TED HEYBRIDGE

summersdale

CONTENTS

INTRODUCTION

They talk of the dignity of work.
Bosh. The dignity is in leisure.

HERMAN MELVILLE, WRITER AND POET

You've heard it said many times, but now you'll see why: *How did I ever find time to go to work?* You're retired, and should have plenty of time on your hands. But with all those long-overdue DIY projects to be tackled, plus the expectation that you can now help with the local fete as well as looking after the grandkids every other day… You might find there's not very much time for merely putting your feet up and twiddling your thumbs – or for following your retirement dreams.

But don't forget that this time is for you.

You've earned the chance to do whatever you've always daydreamed about but never had the time to put into reality. Don't miss your opportunity. Make sure you think about what you really want to achieve – and make it happen. Always wanted to learn Italian, keep chickens, write a novel or spend more of the year in a place you love? Now you have control over how you spend your days, and the sense of freedom can lead to great things.

Physical and mental well-being are the keys to a happy and satisfying retirement. Retirement gives you the leisure to keep health problems at bay by developing your exercise regime and losing bad eating habits you might have picked up during busy workdays. Physical activities will give you energy and positivity.

This is not the time for gaining material things, but for enjoying each day of your life. What you do now will pave the way for the coming decades, so use your time wisely.

Adapting to retirement can, for some, be a challenge that requires effort and patience. It's important to recognise that it's easier for some than others. Don't lose sight of the fact that this is not an end, but the beginning of the next phase of your life.

These days most of us retire brimming with aspirations, ideas and a 'bucket list' of 1,001 things to do, including learning new skills as well as making time for old friends. You won't be alone and it doesn't need to cost the earth. There's a wealth of opportunities out there, and there are more retired people than ever before, feeling younger than ever before. This next chapter of your life could be the best yet.

Retirement is the end of your time as a wage slave, and the beginning of reaping the rewards in a new and exciting phase of life. Not everything in this book will be for you, but I hope it will provide a taste of the potential joys of retirement in store.

CHAPTER 1

THE ACTIVE JOYS OF RETIREMENT

The wandering man knows of certain ancients, far gone in years, who have staved off infirmities and dissolution by earnest walking – hale fellows close upon eighty and ninety, but brisk as boys.

CHARLES DICKENS

In order to have a happy life, a rewarding life, you need to be active.

PROFESSOR RUUT VEENHOVEN, SOCIOLOGIST AND RESEARCHER

OF THE SCIENTIFIC STUDY OF HAPPINESS

Being physically active leads to better health and greater happiness. The level of strenuousness you should aim for depends on your current level of fitness, but retirement is a perfect time to develop an interest in physical activities such as hiking, cycling or gardening – or something a little more unusual like t'ai chi, horse riding or wild swimming. The rewards of exercise are many, and you may discover a new passion.

Moderate exercise makes your immune cells more ready to fight off infection, while releasing those feel-good endorphins that leave you smiling and help you to relax. It also boosts creative thinking, builds self-esteem, releases tension and can be social and fun.

Perhaps you are already physically fit and enjoy sports such as tennis or golf, running marathons or playing football. Now you have a great opportunity to improve your game and could also give something back to the community by coaching younger players or runners. Even if you're not sporty at all, some kind of activity will help break up your week and get you out of the house, as well as improving overall health and aiding sleep.

Exercise and Your Health

Don't underestimate how important exercise is for your health. Physical activity will reduce your risk of these common problems:

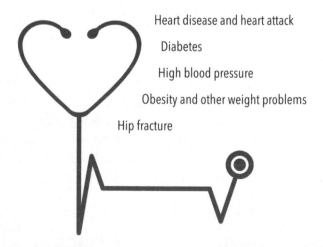

Heart disease and heart attack

Diabetes

High blood pressure

Obesity and other weight problems

Hip fracture

A long-term study carried out by Finnish researchers concluded that those who exercised at a moderate level for at least half an hour a day were half as likely to develop cancer as those who didn't.

Studies have found that the average 65-year-old can increase healthy life expectancy by over 12 years through exercise – and this increases by an additional 5 years if you are highly active. So the answer is easy: find time every day to do something physical.

Team Sports or Solo?

If you find motivation tricky, you may want to choose a group activity that's easy to join in your locality, especially if you're likely to meet group members who'll invite or even encourage you to go every week. On the other hand, perhaps time on your own would be a greater motivator, if that's what you crave: in that case, engaging in a solo sport will become a time of the day to look forward to.

Walk This Way

One of the simplest activities a person can undertake in retirement is to walk. Everyone knows the benefits to be gained in both body and mind merely by opening the front door and stepping outside for a stroll around the block. Extend this to include an amble through the local park or a brisk march along a windswept beach and you are well on your way to developing an all-consuming passion that may well open more doors than you suspect.

Walking is free and full of life-altering potential. Best of all, there are many ways of going about it. If, for instance, the idea of walking alone leaves you cold, consider joining a local group to learn interesting routes and establish new social contacts. Similarly, if the urge to travel strikes you, join a walking tour to some far-flung destination that is not only visually striking but also culturally and historically fascinating.

Established walkers will find that retirement offers opportunities to embark upon lengthier treks than were previously possible. Long-distance footpaths with time and planning offer scope for joyful and possibly even life-changing expeditions. The opportunities are, quite literally, unlimited, with so many routes suited to different capabilities.

Many bookshops cater to walkers with a vast array of guidebooks and more literary works, and some popular walking sites on the Internet include:

 www.walkingbritain.com

 www.nationaltrail.co.uk

 www.nationaltrust.org.uk/visit/activities/walking

 www.ramblers.org.uk/info

 www.walkingworld.com

Walk Away from Stress

The US National Institution for Mental Health and researchers from the University of Kansas found that regular walkers were better able to cope with stressful life changes. For one thing, if you're out walking, you're a lot more likely to meet people than if you're driving a car!

Walks Around Britain

Some of the best walking in the UK is on the national trails; not everyone is ready for a 630-mile (1,013-km) commitment (this is the length of England's South West Coast Path), but you can choose a section of any trail that appeals to you. You can also search for walks depending on your area of interest:

Coast: spectacular coastal scenery is a big attraction around Britain, not least on Scotland's Kintyre Way, Wales' Pembrokeshire Coast Path, England's South West Coast Path, and Northern Ireland's Causeway Coast Way.

Coast-to-coast: the remote Southern Upland Way across the Borders region of southern Scotland satisfyingly starts and finishes at the sea, as do a number of other such walks in Britain.

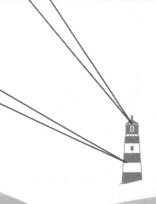

Wildlife: depending on the time of year, on many national trails you can spot orchids and other wildflowers, birdlife and butterflies, and a wide variety of animals – on Scotland's West Highland Way, for example, you could see several species of deer, hares, badgers, foxes, otters and numerous birds of prey including eagle, falcon, osprey and buzzard.

Following in the footsteps of your favourite poet or writer: try the West Sussex Literary Trail, the circuit walk around Tennyson Down on the Isle of Wight, or the Laurie Lee walking trail in Gloucestershire.

Ancient monuments: stone circles, chalk giants and Neolithic burial mounds can all be seen on the Wessex Ridgeway Trail; Offa's Dyke Path has sections of the 1,200-year-old Anglo-Saxon boundary wall; and Hadrian's Wall Path, of course, has Roman remains.

Rivers: at least you can't get lost, and there won't be too many hills, if you follow a river; a selection of river walks can be found at: www.ukrivers.net/walkcycle.html

Mountain scenery: some of the great hikes for this are to be found at Helvellyn in the Lake District and Tryfan in Snowdonia. Check out www.fellwalk.co.uk if mountain hiking is an area of interest.

Refreshments: fortify yourself with cream teas on the Cotswold Way from Bath to Chipping Camden, or with real ale in Yorkshire Dales country pubs on the Pennine Way.

On Yer Bike

What's so good about cycling? Well, first of all, biking around town is a way to save money on petrol and car maintenance, or even on keeping a car in the first place. Or you can give up waiting at bus stops when you embrace the freedom of two wheels. In the meantime, you're doing your heart and body a whole lot of good, naturally. The British Heart Foundation says that cycling 20 miles (32 km) a week reduces your risk of heart disease to less than half that of those who take no exercise. Cycling gets you outside, relieves stress and makes you feel great.

The only problem with biking around town is that you're not always breathing fresh air. That's why you'll soon want to seek out scenic roads where the traffic is light, or off-road bike trails through parks or along canals. Once you get a taste for recreational cycling and develop your strength, you may end up swapping your road bike for a mountain bike. The views just get better if you can tackle a national trail or even an international route. A love of cycling lends itself well to longer routes, so if you're already a keen cyclist, maybe it's time to take on a fresh challenge, such as cycling across an entire country?

I'll Be Off, Then

Fed up with people asking him what he was going to do when he retired from his county council job, Edward Enfield's first act on retirement was to wave them goodbye and cycle across France from the Channel to the Mediterranean, armed only with a tent and a few other essentials. Finding that there's no place from which to see a country that is nearly as good as the saddle of a bicycle, he went on to make cycling journeys around Greece, along the west coast of Ireland and down the banks of the Danube – proving that it's never too late to hit the road. He also found time to write books about the journeys.

Tips for Long Cycling Journeys

- [ ] Travel extremely light; a good bike lock, repair kit and water bottle are essentials, but if you're going to be camping then you'll probably only have space for one change of clothes.

- [ ] If you're travelling alone, make your bike look as unattractive to thieves as possible.

- [ ] Look for scenic old railway tracks that have been developed into cycling trails, and bike-friendly cities, where you'll find two wheels an excellent way to explore.

- [ ] Map out your journey in advance; you might have a smartphone and GPS but are you sure you'll always be able to charge it? Try a solar-powered charger that straps to your back if you need to stay connected.

- [ ] A breakdown is a great way to meet people, but learn some basic maintenance.

- [ ] Be prepared for a change in the weather.

Dance, Dance, Dance

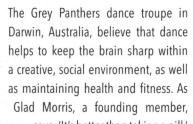

The Grey Panthers dance troupe in Darwin, Australia, believe that dance helps to keep the brain sharp within a creative, social environment, as well as maintaining health and fitness. As Glad Morris, a founding member, says: 'It's better than taking a pill.' With participants predominantly over the age of 60, they are positive role models for being active and productive members of the community, drawing on the long tradition of the 'elder' in the indigenous Northern Territories people.

So how about you? Is there a bit of Cuban fire inside you? Perhaps the glamour of ballroom appeals. Or is it time to come out of the closet as a lover of Morris dancing? Clearly dance is a great way to socialise and keep fit; it can also be a way of deepening your love of another culture if you explore, say, flamenco or Greek dance. To find out what's on near you, ask at your local community centre, council office or municipal health centre, or check out websites such as www.dancesport.uk.com/studios. If you're not ready to dance in public, there are plenty of DVDs available to get you started; though don't forget that in a beginner class, everyone's in the same boat. Dance can burn calories, reduce the risk of high blood pressure, heart disease and diabetes, strengthen your heart and even improve your memory.

The Ex-youth of Today!

Chinese retirees have been seen as troublemakers in cities across the country since they began using the outdoor spaces between apartment buildings for dancing. Using a stereo to play music from traditional folk to love songs to rap, they dance up a storm. It's become quite controversial, as non-participating (often younger) local residents are bothered by the noise and call it a public nuisance. But the dancing retirees say it keeps them active and healthy, and as many as 100 million people – mostly women in their fifties and sixties – now take part, according to China Central Television. Dance leader Tang Keming is quoted as saying, 'It's not only good for physical health, but also for spiritual and mental well-being.' A hundred million Chinese can't be wrong…

Zumba Fitness

Developed originally in Colombia in the 1990s by an aerobics instructor who incorporated some traditional salsa and merengue into a class, Zumba has become a fitness phenomenon that anyone can enjoy. It might take a few classes to master the fancy footwork, but you'll be laughing all the way. A mix of dance and aerobics, typical routines include elements from mambo, flamenco, samba, hip hop and tango, with usually a few saucy pelvic thrusts and hip wiggles, all contributing to a fun workout that tones the muscles. There may be a class that's designed specifically for your age group.

Yoga

Practising yoga regularly can have multiple advantages for health; it strengthens your core, increases muscle tone and improves flexibility, vitality, alertness, balance and breathing. It can also counteract stress and improve mood. It's also very adaptable, depending on your capability, and there are many types to choose from. In fact, retirement is a good time to take up yoga as you have the time to work at it, and its benefits will be valuable in later life.

Hatha is a gentle form of yoga; ideally, find a group specifically designed for your age, but if you can't, then a beginner group is fine. A good teacher will ensure you don't risk injury by moving your body incorrectly. If yoga is popular and there are plenty of practitioners in your area, you could look into Iyengar yoga, which uses props and is considered good for seniors, viniyoga, a form which adapts to the individual, or water yoga.

As Kate Feldman writes on the website www.retirementandgoodliving. com, yoga has changed in the last few decades from something obscure to a practice that's widely accepted as being beneficial for 'physical, mental, emotional and spiritual well-being'.

*While doing yoga we are more ourselves,
and more than ourselves.*

VALERIE JEREMIJENKO, WRITER AND YOGA PRACTITIONER

*Corpse pose restores life. Dead parts of your
being fall away, the ghosts are released.*

TERRI GUILLEMETS, WRITER

Make the Most of Your Gym Membership

Chances are, when you were in full-time employment, you barely got time to dash to the gym and dash out again – back to work, to the supermarket, to be home in time for dinner. Now you have the time to give your gym a proper workout! Instead of leaving straight after an exercise class or session on the machines, go for a swim or indulge in some time relaxing in the sauna, steam room or jacuzzi. Instead of sticking to the same old routines, try some of the other classes on offer, such as Pilates – excellent for strength and breathing – or a dance/aerobics combination.

Try Ayurveda

Ayurveda is a sister science of yoga, and offers a holistic approach to health and wellness. A treatment plan can naturally heal a wide range of illnesses, while an Ayurvedic diet creatively and deliciously helps to strengthen your body's immune system. Full body massages with warm oils are part of the treatment, making it an ideal thing to try while on holiday somewhere warm and serene – especially while getting yourself in shape for the start of your retirement.

Boost Your Brain Cells Too!

Don't forget – your brain also needs exercise to stay healthy. An active brain is able to store and retrieve information more easily. So keep the grey matter fit with any kind of games and puzzles you enjoy – bridge, chess, crosswords, sudoku and cryptograms, or any kind of problem-solving exercise. Boost your brainpower by analysing the stock market or learning a new skill, or volunteer in an area that will broaden your horizons through interaction and new activities, which will benefit your cognitive functioning. Your mind will stay on its toes if you change your habits from time to time – take a different route home or a different newspaper – or challenge yourself with a diverse selection of reading books or audiobooks.

According to the Mayo Clinic in America, physical activity may also help to keep memory loss at bay by increasing blood flow to the whole body – including the brain. Experts agree that the body is able to make neurons, or new brain cells, as the old ones wear out, and that exercise helps those parts of the brain associated with memory and learning. Regular exercise improves cognitive function and reduces the risk of dementia in old age. Stimulating the mind and body, whether through travel, going to museums, volunteering or dancing, will be beneficial for years to come.

CHAPTER 2

THE FINANCIAL JOYS
OF RETIREMENT

*It's nice to get out of the rat race, but you have
to learn to get along with less cheese.*

GENE PERRET, WRITER AND PRODUCER

*Retirement is like… Las Vegas. Enjoy it to the fullest,
but not so fully that you run out of money.*

JONATHAN CLEMENTS, AUTHOR AND SCRIPTWRITER

Retirement can be a great joy if you can find ways to spend your time
without spending all your money. Managing your money is going to
be key to contentment from this point on, as financial worries cause
stress. It doesn't mean you can't do anything ever again – far from it,
as there are endless discounts now available to you.

Think 'streamlining': if you're a two-car household, for example,
consider how necessary that really is, and what you could do with the
money you save by selling one and reducing all your maintenance,
insurance and road tax costs – not to mention the advantages of

travelling under your own steam more often while your partner is using the remaining car. Give up what you don't need to own, in order to do what you'd really love.

Consider also whether you really need a credit card. If you've got a tendency to buy on credit and then incur late-payment fees, maybe it's time to cut up the cards and change your habits. Back when you were working all hours, maybe retail therapy eased your way through the week, but now time is your friend, there are so many better things to do than line other people's pockets. Set yourself financial goals, but make sure there are treats to look forward to.

The Good News

Some people find that they're better off than they ever imagined in retirement. Here are some things you probably don't have to spend money on any more – woohoo!

- Your mortgage
- Your kids' education
- Commuting to work
- Business suits
- Pension contributions
- Lunch at the hated canteen or coffee shop
- High income tax

Goodbye Tension, Hello Pension

You're now getting paid for doing nothing – or, more accurately, for all that work you've done over the years. The only problem is that with so much time on your hands, it's easy to find ways to spend your money. It's likely to be a fixed income, so work out a budget to help you see what you can afford to spend each month.

There's something to be said for delayed gratification. Back when you were working every day, you couldn't go out on 'school nights'. Now you can, but if you go out every night, will you really enjoy it or will you take it for granted? Implement a routine where you budget for a few nights and look forward to splashing out on something you really want on the weekend.

Don't forget to treat yourself to the little things you love in the meantime, especially the simple pleasures that retirement affords. How many times have you bustled out of the coffee shop with a takeaway on the way back to your desk, and envied those who can sit around for hours with a cappuccino and a crossword? Now, that's you!

Budgeting Tip

Download a budgeting template from a money-planning website or see if there's already one installed in the software on your computer. It might be a useful exercise.

Smart Shopping

Now you can visit the supermarket whenever you want, it's about to become a whole lot more fun. For a start, that Saturday scrum is a thing of the past. But not only can you avoid interminable lines at the check-out – you also get to go to your favourite supermarket when items are reduced towards the end of the day.

Other ways to shop sensibly to reduce impact on your wallet include planning your shopping, and making sure you aren't tempted to buy too many extras which might result in food waste. If you're walking or cycling to the supermarket, it's easier to restrict your buying to what you need and not overbuy – you won't be able to carry it home if you do.

It might not come naturally, but sometimes it pays to ask about discounts when buying large items such as furniture. Most vendors are anxious to make a sale, especially when they can get paid in cash. If you ask nicely, you've got nothing to lose.

When buying clothes, think how much wear you'll get out of that new purchase given your current lifestyle. Wait a couple of days and think it over. Just because you like it, doesn't mean you have to have it. On the other hand, if it's something you really love and you know you'll get a lot of wear out of it, it may be a good buy; so if you're sure, go back for it.

Add Up the Ways You Can Save

Simply by introducing some of the activities in this book, you'll be saving cash. For example:

- 💰 Growing your own food and flowers

- 💰 Making dinner at home

- 💰 Cycling or walking rather than driving

- 💰 Selling anything you don't need that's cluttering up the house

- 💰 An interest in birds or wildflowers costs nothing

- 💰 Save on hotels by considering the alternatives

- 💰 Don't skimp on doing a price comparison when buying household items, mobile phone plans or insurance.

Bus-Pass Britain

Depending on where you live and your state pension age, you may be entitled now to a free bus pass. Free bus passes have encouraged a new wave of exploring the country you live in. Bus travel is leisurely, often relaxing if you avoid peak times, sometimes social and, unlike driving, you're free to read a newspaper or book as you ride.

Travel publisher Bradt celebrated the age of the free bus pass with a competition in which members of the public from around the British Isles submitted stories of their favourite bus routes, giving a fresh perspective on places worth exploring. The collection of fifty favourite bus routes, *Bus-Pass Britain*, just might inspire a jaunt or two. Why not take along a friend, and take in a walk, a little sightseeing and a spot of lunch at a recommended pub? Since you're travelling by bus, there's nothing to stop you from having a drink or two…

Have Fun for Free

Most places in the world – even famous cities – offer things to do that cost little or nothing. Whether you're staying at home or visiting somewhere new, why not look up 'free things to do in… ' and get some ideas? Beaches, of course, offer loads of fun for free: swimming, dog-walking, running, fishing, collecting shells and poking around in rock pools. But cities are also rich in cheap treats:

- You're in luck if there's a local festival happening.

- Food markets can be great sources of entertainment, especially if they let you taste.

- Get to know the parks and waterways.

- Observe the different neighbourhoods and get chatting to people.

- Sit in a square in the heart of the town and people-watch.

- Many capital cities have national museums, galleries or botanic gardens with free (or donation-only) entry, while others will offer reduced admission prices for retirees, or may have a free session one evening or during a quiet part of the week.

- Some cities offer free guided tours. If not, take yourself on one by picking up all the free literature you can find at the tourist office, and take a closer look at the architecture and art in cathedrals and churches. If you discover something more about your own home town this way, it can be even more gratifying.

- For a different perspective, climb up the nearest big hill and take in the panoramic view, or, safety permitting, go on a night walk.

Pain-free (and Eco-friendly!) Ways to Save

Turn off electrical appliances and lights when not using them.

Make sure all of your monthly outgoings are necessary.

Renegotiate interest rates.

Make sure you're not paying to heat (or cool) rooms you don't use.

Don't pay for TV you don't watch.

Use a service such as Skype for long-distance calls, so you can talk for free or at least see what you're spending, and cancel phone services you don't really need.

Don't fall for marketing and hype. Do you really need the latest iWotsit? Wait six months and there'll be another latest one.

Consider how much use you're getting out of your gym subscription – with all the extra activities in your life now, you might be better going pay-as-you-go.

Make do and mend.

Line-dry your clothes rather than using the dryer.

Use old rags for cleaning rather than buying cloths.

Does it need to be new? Try online sites such as eBay, Craigslist and Freecycle.

Can you borrow a tool you won't use very often, rather than buy it?

Go Back to Work

We are closer to the ants than to the butterflies.
Very few people can endure much leisure.

GERALD BRENAN, WRITER

It may sound crazy, but retirement doesn't need to mean giving up work completely. You may just want to change the way you work.

Usually after you've been in a job for several years, the cracks in the organisation appear, and you're no longer challenged in the way you were before. There may still be aspects of the work you love, but you wish you had more freedom – the full-time office routine doesn't usually allow you to make the most of the rest of your life. Now you've reached retirement age, you should be able to take a sunny afternoon off to enjoy outside, or take longer lunch breaks to walk your dog. But maybe you still enjoy work. So what's the answer?

Many employers are seeing the value in letting their experienced staff continue part-time after retirement. Other employers may want to keep using your skills on a freelance basis, or perhaps you could branch out into consulting. Pick the days you work, take holidays when you like, do what you want and still have an income – one that's small enough that it won't be heavily taxed.

Location Rebel

Many more young people are retiring early and/or going freelance these days, either because of changes in their industry or their own disenchantment with conventional workplaces. They're developing new types of careers based on what they love. That's the world you're now joining, and it's exciting. While there are other websites available to help you start a new online business, Location Rebel (www.locationrebel.com) goes a step further by allowing you to set goals and encouraging you to join a community.

Start a Consultancy Business

Many of us find in middle age that our jobs are no longer fulfilling us the way they used to; perhaps we've been promoted into management and lost sight of the reasons we went into the job in the first place, or have been passed over for promotion and felt a lack of challenge. Starting your own business can be a way of getting back to doing what you used to love – with the best boss in the world!

Working from home, without the constant interruptions, you'll achieve your tasks in a fraction of the time, and you can set your own goals. According to a study by the London School of Economics, people who work in an office are twice as unhappy as those who work from home – and those earning less tend to be happier, which suggests less stress and doing what you love are the way to go.

Turn a Hobby into a Part-time Job

Turning a hobby into a part-time job can give you the best of both worlds. If you love sewing baby clothes, restoring antiques, baking decadent cookies, fixing gadgets or building garden benches, and would enjoy interacting with customers either through an online site, market stall or retail outlet, your passion could bring in a little pocket money. Whatever you do, a small income from a part-time job can be the equivalent of a substantial amount of savings. And you may enjoy it so much that you never want to retire.

And Now for Something Completely Different

Cornell University psychologists found that men who found another kind of work after retirement were happiest and least prone to depression. Although men are statistically more affected this way, it can of course apply to both men and women.

Money-conscious Tips

If you want to save for a kitchen renovation or a nice trip, here are a few little tricks that might help:

- It may sound cheesy, but why not place a photo in your wallet that reminds you of what you're saving for – whether it's those new cupboards or the place you'd love to go – so you're reminded every time you think of spending on something you might not need!

- Making a spreadsheet or visual chart that shows your progress towards your goal can help, so you're not giving something up, but getting closer to your dream.

- If you have a tendency to impulse-buy, then carry less cash around. If you see something you really want, it'll probably still be there when you go back, and it gives you a 'cooling-off period' to make sure it's something you need.

CHAPTER 3

THE JOY OF NATURE

Nature's peace will flow into you as sunshine flows into trees. The winds will blow their freshness into you, and the storms their energy.

JOHN MUIR, NATURALIST

Come forth into the light of things, let nature be your teacher.

WILLIAM WORDSWORTH

Unless you've been working as a game warden, gardener or postman/postwoman, the chances are that during your average week you were spending far too much time staring at four walls of some kind – and at a computer screen for much of the rest of the time. Perhaps you also sat in traffic for an hour or two a day – or did you suffer the commute by bus or train, trying not to lose your temper with fellow passengers as they talked away obliviously into their mobile phones? In any case, most of us have little enough chance to enjoy the great outdoors while we're working full time.

Yet it has so much to offer. Contemplative time in a garden, park or mountain forest can heal the body and restore the spirits. Once you start stretching your legs, breathing in the fresh air, seeing far and wide, having adventures like kayaking or wild swimming… it may just be that the call of the wild is addictive and you'll only want more.

Nature Studies

Nature is good for body and mind, according to the following studies:

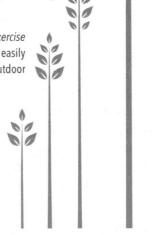

The University of Michigan found that walking for 50 minutes in nature led people to perform significantly better on memory-related tasks compared to results after walking in an urban environment.

A study in Scotland found that people who walked through a rural area 'viewed their to-do list as more manageable than those who walked on city streets'.

Medicine & Science in Sports & Exercise reported that people walked more easily and with more positivity on an outdoor track than on an indoor treadmill.

The journal *Environmental Science and Technology* revealed that as little as 5 minutes of activity in a natural area resulted in improvements to self-esteem and mood.

It's in Our Nature

My heart leaps up when I behold
A rainbow in the sky:
So was it when my life began;
So is it now I am a man;
So be it when I shall grow old,
Or let me die!

WILLIAM WORDSWORTH, FROM 'MY HEART LEAPS UP'

Research continually finds that all of us prefer natural settings over man-made environments. In fact, according to the American Society of Landscape Architects, we are probably programmed by evolution to enjoy landscapes with clean water because of our primal needs, and flowers because 'our ancestral brains know that fruit and seeds come later'. Columbia University researchers found that negative ions, which are abundant near rushing water such as waterfalls, river rapids and breaking waves, can act as natural antidepressants.

So find a long sandy beach and walk along it with your feet in the sea. Now you're retired, you don't have to go on holidays or weekend trips when it's busy. Chase the seagulls, listen to the waves, breathe in all that bracing sea air… Then have fish and chips – you've earned it!

Conservation Volunteers

Conservation volunteers work on environmental projects to help communities reclaim green spaces, and joining a group may well teach you outdoor skills and encourage a fuller appreciation of the countryside. Gardening on a grand scale, it often involves meeting folks of all ages and backgrounds who share a love of nature – and perhaps a social drink at the end of a hard day's work.

In Britain, conservation volunteering began in 1959 with a project at Box Hill in Surrey, where forty-two volunteers – among them David Bellamy – cleared dogwood to encourage the growth of juniper and chalkland flora. Ten years later, an exchange visit to Czechoslovakia's Low Tatra Mountains marked the start of an international programme.

Organisations such as Earthwatch offer international conservation volunteer trips with the opportunity to join research expeditions in exciting protected areas. While the cost can be high, what a way to reward yourself for years of hard work and to kick off your retirement in style – maybe paving the way for years of dedication to a whole new vocation.

Countryside Conservation

Find out what conservation volunteers are doing in your area of the UK at www.tcv.org.uk. Tasks might include:

 Woodland management, e.g. coppicing

 Wetland management

Stone-path refurbishment

Tree planting

Clearing grass from a butterfly meadow

 Hedgerow maintenance

 Uprooting invasive non-native species of plants

 Composting and mulching

Spotting Wildflowers

Not every activity has to be expensive. At its most basic level, indulging a passion for wildflowers can involve nothing more than stretching one's legs. Granted, urban dwellers may find themselves at a disadvantage, although a short bus or train ride is often all that's required to cast oneself into an unsuspected world of singular beauty and complexity. For the fact is that many diverse and fascinating species of wildflowers appear in the most unpromising plots of land. All that's needed to track them down is curiosity and a keen set of eyes.

The quest for wildflowers is, above all, tantalising. In no time at all a mild interest can develop into a full-blown passion, even an obsession; especially as wildflowers appear in a seasonal progression which is repeated annually, invariably in the same places. A vast range of specialist books is available to help identify individual species. There is also, of course, the Internet. The main virtue of wildflowers is that they are beautiful, a gift to the senses. Seeking out and identifying them not only elates the spirit but also hones one's observational skills and involvement with the environment.

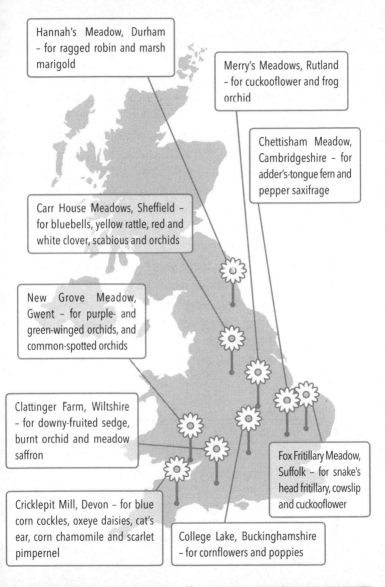

Hannah's Meadow, Durham – for ragged robin and marsh marigold

Merry's Meadows, Rutland – for cuckooflower and frog orchid

Chettisham Meadow, Cambridgeshire – for adder's-tongue fern and pepper saxifrage

Carr House Meadows, Sheffield – for bluebells, yellow rattle, red and white clover, scabious and orchids

New Grove Meadow, Gwent – for purple- and green-winged orchids, and common-spotted orchids

Clattinger Farm, Wiltshire – for downy-fruited sedge, burnt orchid and meadow saffron

Fox Fritillary Meadow, Suffolk – for snake's head fritillary, cowslip and cuckooflower

Cricklepit Mill, Devon – for blue corn cockles, oxeye daisies, cat's ear, corn chamomile and scarlet pimpernel

College Lake, Buckinghamshire – for cornflowers and poppies

Forest-bathing

In Japan, *shinrin-yoku*, or 'forest-bathing' – spending hours in the woods – has been a popular activity since the 1980s, with close to fifty designated Forest Therapy sites listed. But it's only in recent years that research into the very real therapeutic effects, led by Dr Qing Li of Nippon Medical School, Tokyo, has attracted widespread media attention.

Li, a specialist in environmental immunology, has been studying the effects of environmental chemicals, stress and lifestyle on immune function since 1988. He recommends people spend days at a time in the woods to get optimum health benefits, as a treatment to help prevent cancer and lifestyle-related conditions such as heart disease, diabetes, depression and hypertension.

Forest-bathing was originally inspired by ancient Buddhist practice, and the idea is to experience nature through all five senses. In order to enjoy the full benefits, you must leave all electronic devices at home and be present in the moment.

Camp in My Garden

Love camping but can't find a campsite in the place you're visiting? Try www.campinmygarden.com: the world's first garden-camping community!

Fishing

> *A fishing pole is a stick with a hook at one
> end and a fool on the other.*
>
> SAMUEL JOHNSON

Whether or not you agree with
Samuel Johnson, there's no denying the
attraction of fishing. This is a pastime that
allows you to while away hours doing little more than sitting still in
an agreeable place.

Ask a handful of anglers what motivates them and the chances are
you'll receive a wealth of different replies. While actually catching fish is
no doubt the goal of the exercise, it is not the be-all and end-all of this
fascinating sport. Some people go fishing just to get out of the house.
Others seek peace and tranquillity and the opportunity to relax in a great
location. There is also something meditative about fishing that allows us
to forget about worldly cares or turn over ideas on anything from that
night's dinner to the plot of a new novel.

Yet fishing can also be a social activity, providing a golden opportunity
to mingle with like-minded souls. There's nothing like a popular stretch of
river for generating good humour and a sense of camaraderie. You might
also consider joining a fishing club. A love of angling can also take you
farther afield; perhaps you'll be tempted to explore a different location by
planning an expedition across the country or overseas, testing your skills
and introducing you to new environments and ecosystems.

Embrace the Seasons

Was winter your enemy, especially during the shorter days when it was dark when you left for work and even darker when you got home? Outdoors you can rediscover the joys of winter: a morning frost cloaking the trees, crisp bright days or serene mist. Committing to completing a long-distance walk or bike ride – perhaps over a series of winter weekends – will awaken your senses to the pleasures of winter colours in a variety of landscapes, as long as you take care on muddy or icy tracks. You are also much likelier to enjoy peace and quiet, if that matters to you, when fewer people are around.

Join the RSPB

The RSPB protects birds and conducts a wide range of nature conservation. Even buying bird food from the RSPB helps save birds and other wildlife! They also have a full range of binoculars, plus great gift ideas such as stationery and cards. Becoming a member from just a few pounds a month gives you otherwise free access to over a hundred nature reserves – what better way to give the grandkids a great, educational day out? The website is also a useful place to start identifying birds: www.rspb.org.uk.

The Wings of a Dove

There's nothing better guaranteed to awaken an appreciation of the universe in which we live than watching birds. This is also one of the simplest activities a retired person can undertake, the primary requirement for it being the one commodity he or she suddenly has plenty of: time.

Starting in the local park or the garden of your house with nothing more than your two eyes can be amply fulfilling. But, faced with a world you have hitherto been too busy to notice, your curiosity and ambition may well escalate and the purchase of a guidebook and a pair of binoculars may well coincide with the desire to search further afield.

The benefits of birdwatching then begin to multiply with the introduction into your routine of fresh air and exercise. There is also the opportunity to broaden your social network, either by joining a birdwatching club or trusting to serendipity to connect with fellow aficionados whilst out in the field.

On the Lookout

Six top birding days out…

Most famous red kite feeding station – Gigrin Farm, Rhayader, Wales

Top city venue for visiting birds, an easy bus ride from central London – Wildfowl and Wetlands Trust Centre, Barnes, London

Cruise the Exe Estuary in winter to see the avocet, symbol of the RSPB – Exmouth, Devon

See whooper swans, greylag geese and half the UK's goldeneye duck population at a Highlands National Nature Reserve – Insh Marshes, Speyside, Scotland

See the puffins, terns and kittiwakes that make their home on the Farne Islands – by boat from Seahouses, Northumberland

The annual British Birdwatching Fair takes place in August at one of Europe's biggest artificial lakes (and home to ospreys) – Rutland Water, Rutland

For details of birding sites and birds to spot in your area, check out the wonderful resources at www.fatbirder.com

Kayaking

It's better to live one day as a lion than a thousand years as a lamb.
ALEKSANDER DOBA, KAYAK ADVENTURER

When people talk of spending their retirement on a beach in Florida, they don't usually have in mind what Aleksander Doba did. But in April 2014, the 67-year-old adventurer from Poland arrived by kayak on New Smyrna Beach after paddling 6,000 miles (9,656 km) across the Atlantic. He had left Portugal the previous October, and completing the voyage was a dream come true – even though he had barely slept for the entire six months. He had previously paddled a kayak around the Baltic Sea and around Siberia's Lake Baikal.

You don't have to take it to such extremes, however. Kayaking is one of the fastest-growing sports, particularly among people in their sixties and beyond, who tend to favour flat-water kayaking. Kayaks are more stable than canoes and the paddling is easier to master. Areas with plenty of protected bays or marshes are ideal. Sitting peacefully on the water, gliding gently to quiet parts of the coast inaccessible on foot, you're able to get up close to birds, fish and perhaps mammals such as seals. Sit-on-top kayaks are a good option for beginners and those who might have difficulty getting out after a long paddle.

Wild Swimming

The term 'wild swimming' is often understood to mean swimming in natural places, particularly in hidden, wilderness areas where diving *au naturel* is part of the fun. But anyone can enjoy wild swimming in a lake or river – in fact, that's what your ancestors probably did, before public swimming baths became widely available.

Although people have enjoyed wild swimming from time immemorial, in modern Britain we seemed to have lost our connection with wild swimming places due to post-war industrial pollution of the waters, until the concept was reintroduced by environmentalist Roger Deakin from the 1970s onwards. He swam daily in the moat of his semi-ruined Elizabethan farmhouse, and published the book *Waterlog* about his journeys swimming in Britain's waterways, seas and lakes, including river pools in Devon and Wales, the ponds of London's Hampstead and the bays of the Isles of Scilly.

Nowadays, roughly 70 per cent of Britain's rivers are safe again and have become havens of wildlife. Swimming is well known as one of the best forms of exercise, because it uses so many muscles, and wild swimming is about regaining some of that glee we felt as children when plunging into the water, while feeling closer to our natural surroundings. It boosts your natural happy hormones and has multiple accompanying health benefits, including increased libido. We see the landscape differently from the water, and for Roger Deakin it was also an act of defiance to ignore the 'No Swimming' signs and reclaim wild water for everyone.

To find out more, check www.wildswimming.co.uk and www. outdoorswimmingsociety.com.

CHAPTER 4

ENJOYING YOUR
HOME AND GARDEN

Whatever you can do, or dream you can do, begin it.
W. H. MURRAY, MOUNTAINEER AND WRITER

The trouble with retirement is that you never get a day off.
ABE LEMONS, BASKETBALL PLAYER AND COACH

There are many simple joys to be found in your own home: taking a long bath, reading, cooking and gardening, to name but a few. To make the most of your time at home, ensure that it's not a stressful place to be. Remove the clutter, and stock the kitchen with healthy snacks. Think of ways to create an even happier, healthier home where you'll enjoy spending time alone or with friends and family.

However satisfying it is to wake up in the morning and know you don't have to go to work – and it may be so enjoyable that you take a nap for a while just to do it all over again – having more time at home means you may start noticing all those odd jobs and projects that still need doing. There's no need to feel overwhelmed: make a list of priorities, consulting your partner or anyone else who shares the house, and don't feel pressured, as you have plenty of time to complete the job exactly as you want it.

De-clutter Your Life

A large number of us have a clutter problem, and the reasons can be many, according to Kim Carruthers, author of *Less Is More*, including:

- You make a start and it turns into such a major job that the problem seems even worse.

- You've been raised to be thrifty and not throw things away.

- You don't know how long you need to keep records like tax returns.

- You've still got all the kids' clothes, plus the clothes you hope to fit into again one day.

- Emotional reasons can include anxiety, divorce or bereavement.

- Possessions make you feel more secure.

Acquiring stuff, however, doesn't make anything better and the only way to deal with that particular stress is to tackle the clutter and get rid of what you don't need. There's no such thing as a perfect home, but if it's difficult to find things or you don't have any more space, it might be time to address the problem now to give yourself a fresh start and gain control of your home environment to make it a more relaxing place to be.

Here are some tips to start you de-cluttering:

- Share and donate – someone needs it more than you do.

- Only keep what you know you will need.

- Only *buy* what you know you'll need – it may be beautiful, but if you're not 100 per cent sure you'll wear it, don't buy it.

- Borrow or rent rather than buy.

Once you've de-cluttered, you should find that:

Fewer choices about what
dish to cook or what clothes
to wear lead to less stress.

You'll enjoy being at
home more.

You'll spend less time
looking for things.

Ditch Unwanted Magazines

Do you subscribe to a magazine that you never take the time to read properly? Stop the subscription and you'll feel less guilty, have less clutter and save money too.

A Fresh Approach

Unless you want to sell up and move, you may be looking forward to spending a good many years in your home. Making it a more comfortable place will reap many rewards. You'll be happier in simple pleasures and you'll feel more likely to invite people round. Painting a room can make it feel brand new, and when you put back the furniture, experiment by changing a few things, even if it's just the position of the existing furniture. Maybe you've always wanted to convert a room for a different use – perhaps as a hobby room or workshop – or give your home a green makeover. Sit down and sketch out your plans, and jot down ideas about what's important.

What's for Dinner?

Every day holds the possibility of a miracle.
ELIZABETH DAVID, COOKERY WRITER

 With the advent of retirement, the time is ripe to let your culinary pretensions out of the cupboard. The pursuit of excellence in the kitchen can only benefit from the extra time and freedom now at your disposal.

Of course, many people have become expert cooks before they retire. But that doesn't mean that they can't utilise their new leisure time to further their expertise or, indeed, branch out and investigate other, previously unexplored, foreign cuisines. How about mastering Thai curries, or perfecting the pizza?

With the Internet abetting the vast range of specialist cookbooks available, there is no shortage of recipes and cooking instructions. Cooking classes are widely available, should you feel the need for hands-on instruction, while those hankering for a more authentic experience might consider joining a culinary tour to a foreign country. There is nothing more likely to bring a cuisine to life than to visit the place of its origin.

On the home front, make a point of seeking out local produce. Frequent farmers' markets and save money whilst sourcing the freshest and tastiest produce by purchasing what's in season. These gatherings also provide a fund of local lore, not all of it fanciful, and offer the chance to exchange ideas and recipes with other burgeoning chefs.

Start a Dinner Club

Invite a group of friends to try your new culinary creations – and set up dates for the guests to take their turn as hosts. Unless you're all competitive types, avoid one-upmanship and haute cuisine that will put off the less confident. The idea is to have a fun night out, without the prohibitive costs of a restaurant. Putting some thought into music, decor, drinks, games or dinner themes can all contribute to an evening's enjoyment.

Healthy Snacking at Home

If you're going to be spending a lot more time at home with 24-hour access to the kitchen, beware of the temptation to graze on fattening food all day! Make sure you have some celery and carrots to chop up and dip in home-made hummus when you get the munchies. Leftover salads are great snacks, as are edamame beans, berries, porridge, yoghurt and unsalted nuts. If you have a glut of fruit or vegetables from your garden, make fresh juices – much healthier than drinking bought juices, and you can add wheatgrass for extra benefit.

Wise Up on Nutrition

 This is a crucial time to ensure your diet is providing everything you need for future health. Take advantage of this change in routine to read up on what vitamins you need and where you can get them as a natural part of your eating habits, rather than relying on supplements. Maybe you've always been a healthy eater; but research is continually making new discoveries about superfoods. Make sure the balance of nutrients required for your age and lifestyle is incorporated into your routine shop from now on.

The Joy of Gardening

> *I am once more seated under my own vine and fig tree… and hope to spend the remainder of my days in peaceful retirement, making political pursuits yield to the more rational amusement of cultivating the earth.*
>
> GEORGE WASHINGTON

Few pastimes can be as demanding and rewarding as keeping a garden. Throughout the seasons there are different tasks to grapple with – digging, planting, pruning – and different blossoms, leaves and fruits to enjoy. Time spent in the garden gives you fresh air and exercise, and will always result in something to appreciate later, be it a beautiful place to sit or a harvest of organic edibles and flavoursome herbs. If you don't have a garden, then try window boxes and pot plants.

A bird feeder is a fine addition to any garden, attracting more wildlife to help you appreciate the joys of the your own outdoor space. You could even design and build one yourself.

Garden Design

Therefore remember ever the garden and the groves within.
There build, there erect what statues, what virtues, what
ornament or orders of architecture thou thinkest noblest.

ANTHONY ASHLEY COOPER, POLITICIAN

Get inspired to revamp your garden by visiting a show or browsing a magazine or website (for example, see www.gardendesign.com). Perhaps you'd like to create an intimate corner for reading the papers over morning coffee, brighten up an overly shady area, create more colour, plan for variety through the seasons, or become more eco-friendly. A pebble mosaic walkway can be a beautiful feature of your outdoor space and can be achieved on a budget. Look at relevant Pinterest boards to give you ideas. Garden design can become an obsession, but a very healthy one, and perhaps your neighbours will get to enjoy the fruits of your labours too!

> ### *Holistic Gardening*
>
> *On retirement from her 30-year position as a consultant oncologist at Northampton General Hospital, Dr Jill Stewart decided she wanted to use her lifelong love of plants and gardening to design gardens for cancer patients. She began her training in Horticulture and Garden Design at Moulton College after taking Royal Horticultural Society exams, and won first place in a competition run by a local medical centre to design a holistic garden next to the chemotherapy unit.*

Growing Your Own

Growing your own vegetables will cut your grocery bills down radically, and you'll be getting fresh air and exercise for free too. If you don't have space in your own garden, get on the waiting list now for an allotment. Packets of seeds cost very little and you can extend the use of your cultivating skills by learning to pickle and preserve when you have a glut.

Not only is reducing the food miles and packaging better for the environment, but you'll also be picking things when they're perfectly ripe, and the less time your veggies spend in transport, the more goodness you'll gain. The sense of satisfaction when you serve up your own produce is something that can't be bought. And when it tastes delicious, you'll want to eat more. What's not to love?

Lay a Little Egg for Me

If you've got the space, now could be the time to get more ambitious in your self-sufficiency and consider a little animal husbandry.

The keeping of chickens has become wildly popular in recent years and there's any number of books and websites around to get you started. As long as you can keep them safe from predators in their coop, most people find them easy to look after. They'll need food and water and mucking out – even when you go away, so you'll need some helpful neighbours who'll enjoy the free eggs.

Ducks – 'the new chickens', some say – are an excellent alternative as they tend to stay healthier than chickens, are resilient to cold and heat, and lay rich eggs that are great for baking. They tend to be easier on the lawn, and no male ducks make the noise that roosters make. Many people keep both together, although they need slightly different feed.

Love Me, Love My Llamas

'Llamas are like dogs,' owner Pam Fink says. 'They are your friends.'

The llama is 'in', according to *The New York Times*, as an outdoor pet: they're gentle and affectionate and easy to look after, and while llamas were more or less unheard of in the United States a couple of decades ago, there are now about 115,000 of them in that country alone. Many breeders of alpacas as well as llamas are now found around the UK, too – both are traditionally bred for their wool or hair. Why keep alpacas? They're playful, beautiful animals and calming to be around, according to www.amazingalpacas.co.uk. You'll need an acre per two head of llama or five alpacas (visit www. countrywidefarmers.co.uk for more information). That's quite a lot of land, but if you own your own home you could decide on retirement to sell up and move to somewhere more affordable to pursue your dream of keeping animals!

On the Small Side

If you're confined to a small space but still would like some unusual pet company around the home, don't despair! Have you considered a small fish pond for the garden or a terrapin tank for indoor petting? If you prefer fur to fins, then how about a couple of guinea pigs, hamsters, ferrets or chinchillas?

Beekeeping for Beginners

Bees are advantageous for your garden, helping your flowers and vegetables to flourish. Many find beekeeping a fascinating hobby, and the honey is an added benefit, of course. If you end up producing plenty of golden nectar, you could sell it on a market stall or from your front garden – or even learn to make lip balm and other skin products from the wax.

Beekeeping is an ancient art and remains a fine tradition practised around the world. New Zealander Edmund Hillary, who along with Tenzing Norgay became the first to stand on the summit of Mount Everest in 1953, funded his climbing ambitions by helping out with his father's beekeeping business. American poet Sylvia Plath wrote poems about bees while she lived in rural Devon with husband Ted Hughes.

According to the British Beekeepers Association, one in three mouthfuls of the food we eat is dependent on pollination. Yet bees are threatened around the world by changes in the environment, so keeping a colony is good for everyone. Make sure you have the space and it's not prohibited in your area, and consider the initial costs of the gear required. There's no shortage of literature on beekeeping, and books like James Dearsley's *From A To Bee* can take you through the highs and lows of starting out.

Spa Day at Home

*There must be quite a few things that a hot bath
won't cure, but I don't know many of them.*
SYLVIA PLATH, *THE BELL JAR*

There is absolutely nothing wrong with spending two hours in the bath (especially if you've just spent a few hours in the garden, or de-cluttering – it will do your muscles the world of good!). Find yourself a super fragrance, make sure there's plenty of hot water, dim the lighting and have a book or magazine to hand. If you have trees outside your window, open it to the birdsong; alternatively, play a birdsong CD, or put on some soft music. Keep fluffy towels, bathrobe and slippers nearby to slip into when you're ready.

CHAPTER 5

THE JOY OF LEARNING

As long as you're learning, you're not old.
Rosalyn S. Yalow, winner of Nobel prize for medicine

If a man's wit be wandering, let him study the mathematics.
Francis Bacon, scientist and statesman

Many people realise after years in the workplace that there are fewer opportunities for learning, and by the time retirement comes they're longing to devote themselves to a new challenge. Now's the opportunity to continue learning a subject that was perhaps put on hold during your time in the workforce, when financial concerns took priority, or to take up something you've always longed to know more about.

If you need some structure to your day, then setting aside a few hours for learning something new will help you to appreciate the rest of your time. You can maintain a sense of purpose in your life that may otherwise feel lacking now you're not running around fulfilling business duties.

Additionally, by taxing your brain now, you're likely to stay sharp for longer, which means you can continue with a variety of interests well into old age.

Back to School

You're never too old to learn. The wisdom of this age-old maxim has never held truer than in our current day and age, with a seemingly endless range of institutions offering courses in a bewildering array of subjects in many different formats. Whether you want to study informally or add some impressive letters to your name, there is almost certainly someone out there who can help you reach your goal.

Retirement offers the perfect opportunity to study that special subject which you have long been interested in but have never had the time to pursue. Moreover, the benefits of further education go beyond merely acquiring new skills. Continuing education in retirement helps people stay active and interested and thereby promotes both physical and mental health. It also promises to bring you into contact with a broad spectrum of people, the majority of whom will be as passionate and curious about your subject as you are.

Where, what and how you study will depend upon your location and inclinations. Nowadays, universities and colleges offer a selection of learning options including daytime, part-time, weekend and, increasingly, online. Admittance requirements are often flexible, taking a person's work and experience into account. Nor is studying necessarily expensive, with concessions available for mature students.

Step It Up

Researchers believe that, as our learning levels off, the risk of the onset of dementia can increase unless we step up our intellectual activity. Anything that challenges you and expands your knowledge, such as learning a language or starting a new hobby, can be effective.

Don't Slack on Sleep

Did you know that sleep is extremely important for your health? A good night's sleep is essential for preparing the brain for next-day memory formation, and for consolidating what you've learned the day before, according to neuroscientists and the National Institutes of Health in the USA. Napping may also help. During sleep the hippocampus, where memory is stored, moves knowledge from short-term to long-term memory.

U3A

Learning for learning's sake is the philosophy behind University of the Third Age (U3A). This primary goal of this international organisation, which grants no qualifications and offers no assessments, is to provide education and stimulation for people in the 'third age' of life, i.e. the age that follows that of full-time employment and parenting.

The U3A movement began in 1973 in France, where it is usually allied with universities. The academic connection persists on the continent, whereas in Britain, to which the movement spread in the early 1980s, the organisation was altered to a cooperative-type movement run by volunteers. Adopted by other countries throughout the Commonwealth, the British model relies on the skills and life experiences of individual members, which are harnessed and channelled by a group coordinator. Classes are sometimes taught by retired university lecturers.

U3A group sizes vary, according to demand, while between them they offer a wide choice of academic, creative and leisure activities such as art, history, music, languages, life sciences, philosophy, computing, crafts, photography and walking. It's an ideal way to explore an interest without having to sit exams.

Parlez-vous Français?

The limits of my language are the limits of my universe.
LUDWIG WITTGENSTEIN, PHILOSOPHER

A different language is a different vision of life.
FEDERICO FELLINI, FILM DIRECTOR

The idea of travelling more in your hard-earned retirement years is another impetus to knuckle down finally to learning the language of the country you want to discover, thus ensuring you'll make the most of your travel opportunity. If you're thinking of retiring to a European country, then you need to be equipped to cope with legalities and other paperwork, and be ready to make friends with your local neighbours.

There are other reasons to learn a new language. You may want to take Italian classes so you can enjoy opera more, or German to read philosophers in the original language, or Spanish to help you study dance abroad. You may want to further understand your own roots or those of your partner. You may simply love the sound of it.

Language learning is something you can do at your own pace at home with books or online, but joining a class will add another social engagement to your calendar with the accompanying potential to make new buddies. It will also help you keep up the momentum, and there's nothing like learning from a native speaker if your teacher happens to be one.

Carpentry

Working with your hands to build something attractive and practical can be utterly absorbing and ultimately rewarding if you get to enjoy the fruits of your labour for years to come. Carpentry is one of the oldest skills in the world, and the more you learn, the more you can make. You might be able to build anything from shelves to tables to staircases from beautiful pieces of wood, or perhaps even a wooden rocking horse for the youngest grandchild. It's good physical exercise and it maintains your eye–hand coordination. It can also save you money. If you enjoy maths, are naturally detail-oriented and a problem-solver, then a woodworking course at a local college might be ideal for you.

Wine Appreciation

*Drinking good wine with good food in good company
is one of life's most civilised pleasures.*

MICHAEL BROADBENT, WINE CRITIC

*Quickly, bring me a beaker of wine, so that I may
wet my mind and say something clever.*

ARISTOPHANES, COMIC PLAYWRIGHT, *THE KNIGHTS*

If you have an interest in wine, now might be the time to turn it into
a passion. The vast and ever-changing world of wine offers almost
unlimited scope for exploration, contemplation and social contact.

Start by frequenting an independent wine retailer. Offering a
wider and more interesting selection of wines than the average

liquor chain, they will also be able to provide expert advice on things like wine styles, regions and the matching of wine with food. Good merchants are passionate and knowledgeable about wine, and happy, what's more, to pass their knowledge on. Many host in-store tastings, where you can try new wines and exchange thoughts with other like-minded people.

At the same time, consider doing a course or joining a group. You might even form a group of your own to swap ideas with friends and explore older and more esoteric vintages.

Additionally, start taking notes. Describe colours, aromas and the wide spectrum of flavours as the wine crosses your palate. This will not only broaden your enjoyment but also increase your knowledge as you become familiar with different styles and regions.

Augment your discoveries by reading widely. Pick a handful of favourite writers and follow their progress. A good start is Hugh Johnson's *Pocket Wine Book,* which appears annually and is as entertaining as it is informative about regions and vintages across the globe.

Get Online

There was a time that online dating and social media were mysterious things that young people did. Now it's over to you. In 2012 the fastest growing demographic on Facebook was senior citizens, while in 2014 the 55–64 bracket became the fastest-growing demographic on Twitter. Once you've retired from the workplace and are developing new roles and social networks for yourself, you may find yourself at a computer, iPad or tablet more than you ever expected. But if this is new to you, first you'll need to learn what it's all about.

Above all, the World Wide Web is an exciting tool for research, information, ideas and meeting people – and all for the flat fee of an Internet service. Social media such as Facebook are an easy way to keep up with far-flung family members, and you might also find yourself reconnecting with old friends and colleagues. Plus, you can save yourself money by browsing price comparison sites (such as www.moneysupermarket.com) and by buying big-ticket items online, where companies with lower overheads often pass savings on to the consumer.

> ### *Remembering to Use IT (and vice versa)*
>
> *Researchers at the Universidade do Sul de Santa Catarina in Brazil looked at data gathered from over six thousand British adults aged over 50 as part of a study on ageing, and concluded that 'digital literacy', including using the Internet and email, could help to delay cognitive decline and reduce memory loss.*

What's This Twittering All About, Then?

If you've never tried Twitter and only hear about it on the news when some TV celebrity disgraces themselves, you probably can't see the sense in it. But just like any method of communication, it can be used for positive means as well. In fact, used wisely, it can be an excellent way of connecting with people from around the world who share similar interests, from travel to beekeeping.

Up to a fifth of all online adults used Twitter in 2014, according to Pew Research. Especially if you're starting a new business or hobby, you can use Twitter to chat with others about its ups and downs whenever you feel like it. And, as with so many of these social media, it's absolutely free. Don't get caught up in the rush to have lots of followers; enjoy it at your own pace, and if you've got something interesting to say from time to time, people will want to connect with you. The basic steps are:

Choose a 'handle' or user name no more than fifteen characters long – this may be your real name, but you may want to focus on your particular interest, and come up with something playful and casual such as @bees_are_best if you're a beekeeper, or @potatohead if you want to share potato-growing tips!

Write your profile in a snappy way that will make people laugh or intrigue them. Twitter, you'll soon learn, is about saying something fast in as few words as possible. Browse through other people's profiles to get a sense of what you think works best.

Make a few 'tweets' – messages in 140 characters or less. Let people get a sense of you through what you say. Tell people what you want to talk about. You can use a 'hashtag' to highlight the topic of your discussion, which will make it easier for people with similar interests to find you. Ask questions, e.g. 'Any good tips about how to keep pests away from potatoes? #garden #veg'

Post funny or beautiful photos. Give tips and information. Make your newsfeed something that people will see value in following - something they might want to share with their friends.

When you're satisfied it all looks good, start looking for people you'd like to connect with, and 'follow' them. If they like what you're doing, they may follow you back. Ignore or delete any that look like 'spam' - people who are clearly trying to sell you something, or photos of scantily clad ladies who profess to be feeling lonely…

Grow your little network gradually and soon you'll have a stream of messages every day that should provide you with information and/or entertainment.

Facebook

Facebook still tops all the social media in terms of general use by men and women of all ages, far outranking relative newcomers such as Instagram and Pinterest. It's easier to use than Twitter as you don't have to restrict what you say to 140 characters, and most of us connect well with visuals, so Facebook seems to be a good all-rounder. Remember the days when we used to print out holiday photos and pass them around over a cup of coffee? Now you download them from your camera straight to your computer, take out all the ones that didn't work out quite as you'd hoped, and load the best onto Facebook – or upload them straight from your smartphone – for all your friends to browse through at their leisure. Sure, there are continual scares about how Facebook uses what you put on there, and you should protect your privacy and other people's, but what we enjoy about Facebook seems to outweigh the negatives. So if you're not on there yet, why not sign up and see what you've been missing?

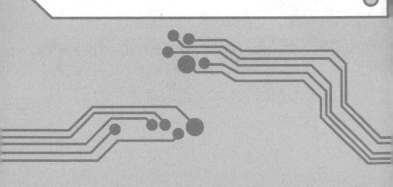

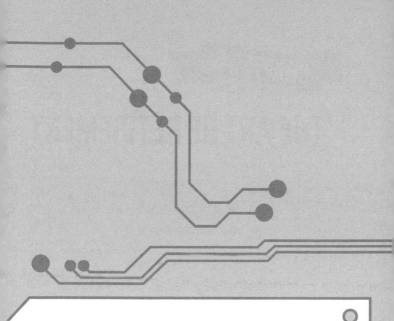

Learn to Promote Your New Venture

If you're thinking of turning your hobby into a business or want to publish your own book, why not take a course in online marketing? Online is the cheapest way to connect with people who might be interested in what you're doing – 'soft' marketing rather than hard sell – and a course will provide you with the tools you need such as Search Engine Optimisation, Blogging, Pay Per Click Advertising and Social Media. You can also learn how to make your business stand out from the competition, understand your target market and monitor your marketing activities to see what works. A small-business masterclass to learn from those who know could be invaluable.

CHAPTER 6

THE ART OF RETIREMENT

There's nothing like the daily grind of work to stifle the artist that lurks within us.

KELLY GREENE, JOURNALIST

All intellectual improvement arises from leisure.

SAMUEL JOHNSON

Retirement can be a wonderful time to allow your love of the arts to flourish by visiting a wide range of museums and exhibitions, and attending concerts and author talks. It may also be your chance to unleash your creativity and express yourself more deeply than ever before. Whatever your chosen medium, you'll have more time and energy to devote to it now that you're no longer pouring your soul into work. Always wanted to pursue your love of classical guitar or write a novel? Now is your chance.

'People often set interests or opportunities aside on the way out the door to pay the mortgage,' says psychologist William Winn. But taking up artistic pursuits now, from picking up an instrument to throwing clay to treading the boards, may bring out something in you that you never even dreamed existed. Once again, a sense of dedication and achievement as well as meeting new people and finding a new passion are all potential benefits. It could even turn into a new career that might not pay as much as your last one but is more deeply rewarding.

The Energy of the Arts

It's well recognised that art and music touch us so deeply that they can have therapeutic effects to help people recover from tragedy and trauma. Doing something creative helps us find solutions to our problems. If retirement has been a big step, particularly if you didn't retire by choice, then you may have energy that could be positively channelled into the arts.

Painting for Pleasure

'I think he's a better artist than he was a president,' commented 81-year-old Beverly Shaver in the *Chicago Tribune* when George W. Bush's exhibition of paintings went on display at the Evanston Art Center in 2014. Bush's decision to pursue his love of painting in retirement got the thumbs-up from fellow retirees following similar artistic passions. 'I love the passion he's got for it,' commented 78-year-old Judy Edelman. 'He's a more interesting person than he appeared when he was president.'

Painting is often a pleasure that's set aside when people are consumed by the requirements of career and family. But it's a joy to come back to in later life, partly because it's such an absorbing activity that demands focused concentration for hours at a time. Barbara Heaton, 67, says, 'It's about the process, not the product.' It's also something you do entirely for yourself, and is therefore good for you.

Signing up for an art class is an ideal way to get the creative juices flowing, but of course it doesn't have to be painting – it could be sculpture or pottery or drawing, for example, or perhaps cartoons or photography are your forte, and there are plenty of good books and DVDs available if you'd rather do it privately. A holiday with a focus on art is a great way to see a place and make friends.

Ten Great Museums for Art Lovers around the UK

Tate Britain, London – a great Turner collection, plus Picasso, Blake and much more

Arnolfini, Bristol – one of Europe's leading centres for contemporary art, with a wide variety of events

British Museum, London – a feast of art and culture from all over the world, its permanent collection has some eight million works

The Henry Moore Institute at Leeds Art Gallery, Leeds – wide-ranging exhibitions on historic and contemporary sculpture

Walker Art Gallery, Liverpool – Rossetti, Monet and Hockney, fun activities for the grandkids and free entry

The Burrell Collection, Glasgow – Rodin, Degas and Cézanne as well as medieval art, in a woodland setting

Scottish National Gallery, Edinburgh – includes must-see works by Botticelli, Constable, Rubens and Rembrandt

The People's Gallery of Murals, Belfast – the Bogside Artists' record of the area's troubled history since 1968

Bodelwyddan Castle, Rhyl – home to the National Portrait Gallery in Wales, set amid Denbighshire parkland

Birmingham Museum and Art Gallery – largest public Pre-Raphaelite collection in the world, plus the jewellery from the Anglo-Saxon Staffordshire Hoard

Ten Great Museums for Art Lovers Worldwide

State Hermitage Museum, St Petersburg, Russia

Guggenheim Museum, Bilbao, Spain

Museum of Bad Art, Boston, USA

Museum of Cycladic Art, Athens, Greece

Uffizi Gallery, Florence, Italy

Egyptian Museum, Cairo, Egypt

Vitra Design Museum, Weil am Rhein, Germany

Fondation Maeght, St Paul de Vence, France

National Museum of Anthropology, Mexico City, Mexico

Metropolitan Museum of Art, New York, USA

Room for Reading

Retirement is traditionally your time to work through the classics of literature that you never had time for. But maybe you'd prefer to discover a whole new genre. You may feel you're well read in contemporary literary fiction, but there's a world of biography that you've barely touched upon, for example. If you're planning to write, you'll need to read widely in the genre to which you want to contribute until you're familiar with what readers want. If you're starting a new hobby or want to learn more about a health condition affecting you or your family, there may be a section of the library just waiting for you.

Books and Book Clubs

You can also give your reading some focus by joining a book group. Perhaps there's already a local book club or one run through the library, or maybe you and your friends would consider starting one. Being part of a book group helps you to discover literature and gives you an opportunity to discuss it with others before you move on to the next tome. Ideally, you'll find you think more about what you're reading and ultimately get more out of it.

Publishers love reading groups, and some will offer discounts on books or extracts to download when you're choosing your next book. The online site www.readinggroups.org can help you find a club near you in the UK and has offers and tips, while www.lovereading. co.uk is a lively site full of ideas and recommendations. Another way of learning about new books, reviewing them and discussing with others is the online site www.goodreads.com.

Subscribe to **The Oldie**

Now there's nothing to stop you reading The Oldie, *one of the most entertaining magazines around, set up by Richard Ingrams after he retired from editing* Private Eye *as 'an antidote to youth culture', focusing on quality writing and illustration, with plenty of humour. More than a magazine,* The Oldie *hosts literary lunches in London and runs writing courses.*

Writing a Book

Have you always thought you've got a novel in you? Or maybe it's a memoir, or a guide to your particular field of expertise? Writing a book can easily take months if not years, and that's just the first draft. But if you feel the creative urge, the good news is that now there's a wealth of resources to be found online to help you through the processes of getting feedback on that first draft from fellow writers, finding an editor, and publishing the book.

Publishing Your Own Book

Writing and publishing a book is deeply satisfying on many levels: the commitment involved in setting down your words, rereading them and rewriting them; the collaborative process of working with an editor; the interaction later with readers.

Traditional publishing is only one of the options available to writers. There was a time when publishing your own book was seen as 'vanity' publishing, but now it's all the rage. In fact, these days even authors with traditional publishers have to learn to enjoy the process of promoting their own work and learn about book marketing. So, particularly if you're writing a practical book that will sell to peers with similar interests, you could look into the costs and rewards of going it alone. Many authors get frustrated with the process of sending out their work to publishers and agents, only to receive a rejection. By self-publishing, you retain control and can work with freelance editors and design professionals to ensure you're 100 per cent happy with the end product.

Online sites where you can share your writing and get feedback to help you improve, or self-publish online for minimal costs:

- [ ] Authonomy
- [ ] Ether Books
- [ ] Wattpad
- [ ] Smashwords
- [ ] Lulu
- [ ] Completely Novel

BLOG IT

A good way to practise your writing skills and build up an online audience for your future book is to start off with a blog – or maybe blogging is your vocation. You get instant gratification from seeing your new blog published, and feedback from your followers. Recipes, photography and travel are all popular topics – as are book reviews.

Never Too Old

Don't let anyone tell you it's too late to start writing. Charles Bukowski didn't publish his first novel until he was 51. Laura Ingalls Wilder didn't publish Little House on the Prairie *until she was 64.*

Melody Maker

Writer Diane Cole went back to playing the piano at the age of 50 after the death of her husband. She had learned piano as a child, but found her fingers too occupied with computer keyboards during the decades of work. When she needed to give her life a boost, however, the love of piano was still there. As her old piano teacher used to say to her, 'If you play the piano, you'll never be bored.'

If playing music used to give you pleasure, retirement might afford you the time to relax and enjoy practising again. (Now may be the time to convert that extra bedroom into a soundproof studio…) Lessons to get you started can be sourced via a music shop or school, community centre or continuing education college, or even better, by recommendation from a friend. The importance of finding an inspiring teacher is vital.

Making Sweet Music

Researchers believe that the mental stimulation of learning a musical instrument can keep memory loss at bay. Making music can also be a very social experience, especially if you're already good enough to play for others. Have you thought of starting up a band with some acquaintances, and writing your own music together, or even playing local gigs? If you need a bit of practice, an old people's home might be very grateful of some lively entertainers!

Bell-ringing

How soft the music of those village bells,
Falling at intervals upon the ear
In cadence sweet; now dying all away,
Now pealing loud again, and louder still,
Clear and sonorous, as the gale comes on!
With easy force it opens all the cells
Where Memory slept.

WILLIAM COWPER, FROM 'THE TASK'

Campanology: the art of ringing the changes. Doesn't it sound lovely? Well, it does if you learn how to do it properly... Bell-ringing is an ancient art and an unusual hobby, but could ap-peal (ouch!), especially if you are already involved in the church, interested in history or simply lucky enough to live near a particularly beautiful and venerable cathedral. The website www.bellringing.org can connect you with ringers all over the UK. Bell-ringing is performed entirely from memory, and is also a very physical form of music-making. Besides being a community activity, it can lead to great opportunities to visit new places.

Join a Choir

*Even the odd off-key note or wrong lyric can't detract
from how good singing makes me feel.*

SARAH RAINEY, FEATURES WRITER, *THE DAILY TELEGRAPH*

If you love singing, joining a choir can be a way to let loose your creative potential in a happy learning environment, with the chance to encounter people from all walks of life. Singing together has been an important part of worldwide culture throughout history and yet so seldom do we get a chance to express and enjoy ourselves this way in modern society.

It's practically impossible to feel stressed when you're singing for fun. Science has proven that it releases endorphins that make us naturally happier, healthier and smarter. Researchers at the University of Gothenburg, Sweden, found that singing in a choir can have a calming effect that is as beneficial to health as yoga. Naturally, it's also good for the lungs, and the *Journal of Music Therapy* reported that it helps patients cope with chronic pain.

Amateur Theatre

Many communities have a theatre group that puts on performances. If you enjoy drama, this might be a chance to get involved. Start off by volunteering behind the scenes with costumes, sets or even selling tickets if you like contact with people (this should allow you to see shows for free). Alternatively, seek out a 'senior theatre' group where you'll make new friends and where there might be more scope for acting opportunities. If you have a background in performing or have always wanted to audition for a role, ask around to see what the procedure is within the group.

Making a Song and Dance about Retirement

A cabaret of song and dance performed by a theatrical group in Darwin, Australia, called *Reluctant Retirees*, traced the journey of two women about to retire. One looked forward to the happy work-free days; the other feared a loss of identity once she lost the connection with her workplace. In the end, both found there was never enough time to do everything that retirement offered.

Craftmania

Crafting has become hugely popular among all age groups in recent years, so you might be surprised to find an array of interesting resources on knitting, crochet, quilting, scrapbooking, designing clothes or making cards. Indulge in some long-neglected pastimes, and create things that will give you pleasure. Learning a craft is in itself mentally stimulating and provides great satisfaction.

If you have a knack for making one-of-a-kind creations, you could join thousands of other amateur crafters who sell what they make on Etsy or Folksy, online sites for buying and selling handmade items from jewellery to stationery, and perhaps earn a little income to pay for your supplies. Pinterest is another online site that's full of inspirational ideas.

Designing and making something personal for someone for their birthday or Christmas means so much more than buying an impersonal item from a shop. Would someone you know love a cushion covered in doggie prints or bicycles, or any design based on their favourite activity? Make something fun!

Some of the Crafts Sold on Etsy and Folksy

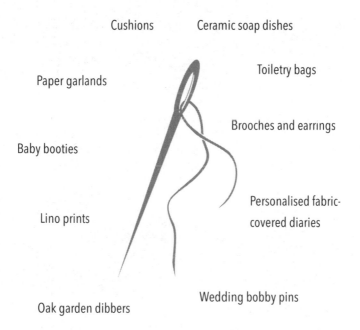

Cushions   Ceramic soap dishes

Toiletry bags

Paper garlands

Brooches and earrings

Baby booties

Personalised fabric-covered diaries

Lino prints

Oak garden dibbers   Wedding bobby pins

Top Ten Films to Watch in Retirement

And finally, when you just need to put your feet up at the end of a long, hard day being retired, here are some top films to inspire you to even greater things the next day:

 The Best Exotic Marigold Hotel

Romantic comedy about a group of pensioners moving to a retirement hotel in India. Its many stars include Judi Dench and Maggie Smith.

Newly retired and widowed Warren Schmidt (Jack Nicholson), feeling a lack of purpose, begins a search for a new life in the Winnebago he and his wife had planned to use in retirement.

 **About Schmidt**

 As Young As You Feel

A printer, forced to retire at age 65, dyes his hair black and poses successfully as president of the company.

Starring John Wayne, an American boxer who retires to the village in Ireland where he was born, hoping to find tranquillity. He finds love with Maureen O'Hara.

 **The Quiet Man**

A poignant caper film about three senior citizens who decide to give up their days of reading newspapers and feeding the pigeons on park benches in favour of a bank heist.

Going in Style

My Retirement Dreams

Documentary about America's way of growing old, following retirees in Miami struggling to leave behind their old lives and find new meaning.

Comedy drama set in a home for retired musicians. Its stars include Michael Gambon, Billy Connolly and Maggie Smith (as a bad-tempered old opera singer in need of a hip replacement).

Quartet

The Bucket List

Two terminally ill men, played by Jack Nicholson and Morgan Freeman, meet in hospital and set out together to achieve all the things they still want to do.

Grumpy London pensioner Arthur (Terence Stamp) honours the memory of his recently deceased wife Marion by joining her choir, and embarks on a journey of self-discovery.

Unfinished Song

Calendar Girls

If you're thinking of raising money for charity, this comedy about a group of Women's Institute ladies in Yorkshire might give you some ideas…

THE JOY OF RELATIONSHIPS

Lord save us all from old age and ill health and a hope tree that has lost the faculty of putting out blossoms.

MARK TWAIN

Here's a piece of good news: simply spending time with friends and relatives is good for you.

Talking on the phone or getting together for a chat is actually mental exercise that helps keep you sharp and can lower your blood pressure. (Gents, you're the ones who have to work at this; ladies, talk as long as you like…) Socialising has actually been proven to be just as effective as crosswords at boosting your intellectual prowess. So a new hobby that involves meeting people can do you the world of good. Even if you're just going to the gym or walking the dog, why not invite someone along?

Retirement is not only a good opportunity to consolidate friendships, but you can spend more time doing things with your partner and really get to know the grandkids. You could have some surprises in store. Retirement may allow a more sociable and compassionate you to develop. If you don't currently have a partner and are feeling lonely, the opportunities for meeting someone with similar interests are just about to begin.

Giving

Is there anyone in your family who could use a bit of help? The older family members might need some help around the house or garden. The younger ones might need some help with the kids. Offering to help them out will at least give you a warm glow, and besides, you'll get to spend more time with them.

De-stress with Friends

Retirement can be a wonderful time for spending more time with loved ones and with good pals. Toronto-based psychotherapist Judi Siklos says socialising with friends 'is one of the most important things you can do to combat stress'. Researchers at the London School of Economics found that people's moods improved the most when they were with friends; however, just as you'd expect, happiness does not increase with the number of friends, but depends rather on the quality of time spent with them.

Now that you're removed from the network of colleagues, supportive friendships will become more important. It's also vital to be able to share your emotions with others as you adjust to the life change of retirement. Companions can help you cope.

Love and Marriage

Who knew your other half had such annoying habits? Just as well you don't have any...

You've most likely never spent so much time together. It's a joy, but it's also terrifying when you think about it, isn't it? Assuming at least one of you worked outside the home, you're probably used to spending about 6 hours a day in one another's company. If you double that in retirement, there's bound to be tension from time to time. Do you have common goals for retirement – and if not, will you support one another's dreams either by joining the other or spending some time apart?

Make sure you have separate interests and see your own friends. That way, you'll have something to talk about when you get home. On the other hand, this may be a great opportunity to do a renovation project or start a business together, and see your partnership develop in an exciting new way. Be gentle with your partner if one of you retires first – the chances are, it's not as easy as it looks for the other half.

Communication

Things to bear in mind if you're sharing your home with your partner...

☎ Proper communication between you and your partner is more important than ever now; it's not so easy to walk away from an argument when you're at home together for longer.

☎ Be aware of how your partner and you are feeling. Does one of you appear to be depressed by retirement? Is one of you trying to be 'boss'? Have you divided up the household chores to everyone's satisfaction? Instead of bottling up concerns, talk to each other about them.

☎ If there are problems in your relationship, they will need to be addressed and fixed – otherwise they will get worse.

☎ You both need to be ready to listen, and to assert your own needs calmly and clearly.

☎ You should feel free to have your own space and do your own thing; if you feel your partner is being dismissive of your new interests, think about how to communicate why they are important to you.

☎ Financial decisions that affect you both must be discussed.

☎ If any of these things are difficult for one or both of you, Michael Longhurst's book *The Beginner's Guide to Retirement* walks you through tackling such tricky territory step by step, with exercises.

Quality Time

Perhaps you haven't always been 'there' for all the people in your life, at least not as much as you'd like. You may have had to miss family events in the past because of work commitments. Your partner understood why you couldn't always have dinner together. Your friends knew you were busy. But now that time's on your side, make sure those you care about are aware of it, and make up for lost time if necessary.

Take the time to call, or email, or visit. Connect with people now, before it's too late and they've moved on. Invite them to do something with you – perhaps a walk in the botanic gardens, or a visit to an exhibition, or watching a film. Make sure you choose something you think they'd enjoy, and don't make them feel pressured if they have commitments. Let them know you're available.

Getting together with friends needn't mean an expensive night out. Just as wasting money has become unfashionable in business since the recent economic crisis, similarly splashing money around in a social setting has less appeal these days. If your friends are also retired, they should understand that it's the meeting up that's important, not the latest trendy venue.

Being a House-guest: Tips to Ensure You'll Be Invited Back

If your grown-up children, relatives or good friends live far away, wouldn't it be great to have more than a phone call or Facebook message, and actually go and visit? Keep in mind that they probably want to see you but may have busy lives themselves. Some general tips to keep in mind…

Try to keep similar hours to your host.

Choose a simple but useful gift.

Leave things as you found them when it's time to go home.

Buy some groceries to help cover the cost of your stay.

Pitch in with things you notice that need to be done, like washing up or walking the dog.

Prove you can spend time on your own and don't always need entertaining.

If they don't wear shoes inside the house, ask if you should remove yours.

And of course, even if you've spent half the time doing their chores and looking after their kids, don't forget to say thank you...

Good Grandparenting

I never had the time before to notice the beauty of my grandkids.
HARTMAN JULE, WRITER

Grandparents have a huge influence on children. Because you don't boss them around or impose all the rules, they're more likely to bond with you. If their parents work long hours, they could probably use some additional guidance and adult company. So take the time now to get to know your grandchildren. Your relationship with them can be one of the most satisfying things in your life.

Perhaps you'll be the one to teach them to ride a bike, help them with a school project or take them to a national park to look for wildlife. If they live far away, get into using Skype so you can chat face to face for free, even when you can't be with them. They can probably teach you how to use it if you're new to the medium!

Ten Things to Do with Your Grandkids

1 Introduce them to books you think they'll love – and even better, take them to the library to introduce them to the joy of choosing books.

2 Get them giggling with a few jokes (you can actually download a free book of jokes for young kids from the www.grandparents.com website).

3 Paste together a scrapbook.

4 Build a model.

5 Plant a treasure hunt around the house or garden.

6 Show them that doing a good turn for someone can be rewarding.

7 Encourage them to create a play or a music routine to perform.

8 Teach them how to make a cake or a pie.

9 Let them get messy with papier mâché, or a sculpture from the recycling bin.

10 Help them to write/draw a family tree.

Researching Your Family History

The chances are that by the time you retire you are aware of more than a few ghosts in the family cupboard. Now, with the necessary time at your disposal, you might feel tempted to drag them out into the light of day. Writing your family history is fun, thought-provoking and deeply satisfying, but if you don't particularly like writing, you could design a visual map or even make a video retelling your findings. There are no hard and fast rules about how you record the fruits of your research. If you do like the idea of having a written account but don't know where to start, you might consider doing a writing course in the genre in order to help you record what your investigations have uncovered.

The obvious place to start is with your living relatives, the older the better. Hopefully they will appreciate your interest and enjoy the opportunity to talk about their memories. Possibly this interaction might lead to you developing friendships with long-lost connections or those with whom previously you only had passing contact. If the final story you piece together would be of interest to the rest of the family or to future generations, perhaps you'll want to make a few printed copies.

How to Do the Research

Seek out photograph albums, diaries and letters, from as many sources as possible.

Scrapbooks, memorabilia collections, old school reports – it is all grist to your mill; use these to find common points of interest and develop an angle on the story you want to tell.

Look for the telling details, the elusive facts. You are, in a sense, a detective, uncovering meaning in a murky past.

Your subjects are real people who have led interesting lives. Military records, records of service in occupations such as the merchant navy, and even, in more lurid cases, prison records are waiting to be explored.

National libraries are full of useful information, as are census and immigration records.

Search online, both to access information and to utilise the available resources.

Social networks like Facebook and Twitter will help you make useful and, at times, unexpected connections.

Joining a family history society might also prove useful.

Companionship

If you live alone and just haven't met a special someone for some time, don't let yourself get lonely. Do make an effort to make new friends if old ones move away. Reach out to others and find activities that involve social contact such as a book or bridge club. If the house feels too big, you might consider getting a lodger or even house-sharing with a trusted friend.

But if you're one of the many who would like to find something more romantic, then don't fall into the trap of thinking you've left it too late. It's hardly unusual to find yourself 'back in the game' after retirement these days.

Think of all those hours you used to spend at work. Those same hours can now be filled with activities you love. Meeting people in a group is far easier than one on one. While you're pursuing your passion, the chances of finding a true soulmate rise exponentially. So get out there and follow your dream, and see where it leads. If your retirement plans involve travel, why not try a singles holiday?

City Life

City life can be better if you're single and retired. Why? There's so much to do that's easily available in a city, from museums, cinemas and theatre, art events and university courses – all free or discounted for seniors – to coffee shops and good-value eateries, and of course a wider variety of people with whom to interact.

Finding Love Online

Don't cringe: Internet dating has come a long way. The fastest-growing sector using online dating sites is yours – midlife and beyond – and some sites are especially made for the fabulous over-fifties and super over-sixties (e.g. www.ukmaturedating.com). Ask around to see if any of your friends have enjoyed using a particular site. Try to find one where people's profiles seem honest. Sometimes fees to join a more exclusive site can pay off because they have better filters.

Finding a site that pitches itself as a 'friendship and dating site' can make the chatting online more fun. By making it clear you're interested in social friends as well as dating, there's no pressure if you like someone but don't see them immediately as a potential mate. The upside of Internet dating is that you never know who you might meet – they might have similar goals to you, they could have had a fascinating life, but you might never have met them otherwise. You might find a new friend or two with a similar sense of adventure.

Safety First

Find a site you trust and beware of scams. Don't put yourself in a dangerous situation by agreeing to meet a total stranger somewhere that's not public, or telling them where you live or giving away too many personal details, however nice they appear. If you follow the simple rules of safety – and you'll find them online – then there's nothing to lose.

CHAPTER 8

THE JOY OF GETTING AWAY FROM IT ALL

Retire from work, but not from life.
M. K. SONI, WRITER

Come, my friends,
'Tis not too late to seek a newer world.
ALFRED, LORD TENNYSON, FROM 'ULYSSES'

Perhaps the biggest retirement goal is travelling. No longer confined to short holiday periods fitted in around your working life, you might want to consider doing something more ambitious. You could take a longer trip, whether abroad or close to home, and don't have to worry about getting back to a pile of paperwork.

For many people, the dream is already firmly in place as they wave goodbye to their old colleagues: time to hop around the Greek islands with no imminent flight home, or go volunteering in Sri Lanka for a few months. On retirement from the BBC, journalist David Treanor decided to drive a van to Mongolia with a friend to raise money for charity.

The key is to keep it relatively cheap – aided by the fact that you can now be flexible on travel dates and pick up discounts. Make the most of it by finding the right means of travel for you, and knowing what you want to get out of it.

A Holiday from What?

If you're not working, why do you need a holiday? There are many reasons why getting away can increase your happiness level during retirement and give you fresh energy:

Taking on new challenges and having unexpected new experiences

A break from routine that may encourage you to break with habits

Fun and laughter away from your everyday environment

Learning new things about the world and yourself

Making new friends

Pushing your boundaries

A new perspective on your life

No longer taking things for granted

Setting new goals and evaluating your life

THE JOY OF RETIREMENT

Airbnb

Airbnb.com is an online site that allows you to rent unique places to stay – usually a room, apartment or entire house, but there are also windmills, lighthouses, treehouses, yurts, boats, castles and private islands… You can even stay in John Steinbeck's old writing studio, or the old workplace of Charles Dickens (though it is somewhat changed).

You rent direct from the owners and, at its most basic, it can be a way to stay affordably in an interesting place. Some set-ups allow you to meet your hosts, who are proud to show off their interesting home and their corner of the world. One great benefit of airbnb is that you're staying in an actual neighbourhood rather than a hotel surrounded by other tourists. So you live like a local; there might be a local market nearby and neighbourhood restaurants. Often you have access to a whole home, meaning it's perfect for longer stays; you'll have a kitchen, and maybe a collection of books to borrow from while there.

To offset your costs – though airbnb properties are usually cheaper than hotels – you can list your own home on the same site. It's easy and it opens up a whole new world of adventures. If you're not sure where you want to go but love the idea of something different, search out where the best bargains are to be had. Just browsing the site is bound to give you a travel bug!

Happy House-sitting

Discover the world of house- and pet-sitting, where you can get to know a new place absolutely free – except for the fee of signing up to a website. All you have to do is look after someone's home, garden and pets while they're away. If you're feeling the need for a change of scene, and if you're a capable person who loves animals, the world is your oyster now with a range of sites where you can search for assignments and apply for them.

The most exciting part about house-sitting is that it offers a way to stay in a place you'd love to go. You could hunt for house-sitting assignments on a Mediterranean island or a beachside town in Mexico; find yourself a mountain retreat in France or an eco-cabin in the Adirondacks. As long as you can prove you're a responsible individual or couple with an aptitude for maintaining a property, these places can be yours to enjoy for a while. It's travel without the cost of accommodation or eating out. Homeowners often specify that they're looking for a retired person, as they want a mature, capable person who's likely to spend time with their pet rather than go out to work.

Sites include www.mindmyhouse.com and www.nomador.com, and plenty of local sites such as www.aussiehousesitters.com and www.housesittersuk.co.uk.

Pet Love

One of the main reasons people want a house-sitter is to look after their pets while they're away. Befriending animals is part of the appeal: having a dog forces you outside for exercise and is wonderfully social as so many people will want to meet the pooch you're walking. An animal's companionship and love is, of course, a reward in itself.

Motorhome Magic

The first Touring Landau was shown at Madison Square Garden auto show in 1910, and now the range of motorhomes available from the basic to the very plush is mind-boggling. But be it an RV (recreational vehicle), housebus, Winnebago, or just a little caravan or campervan, this is your ticket to being at home wherever you are on the road – and being free to go wherever you like.

Embrace the inner hippie and take off with your guitar and a pile of books, or just a heap of curiosity and an open mind. With a motorhome you can stay in a campsite right on the edge of the wildest stretch of coast, and still have all your creature comforts. Well, some of them, at least…

If you love travelling so much that you want to spend more of the year on the road, websites such as www.caniretireyet.com offer invaluable tips on how to choose your RV, minimise the running costs and live better with less. If you like the idea of caravan/motorhome camaraderie, join a club such as www.retiredcaravanners.org.uk.

Details, Details

If you decide to stay on the road for more than a few weeks at a time, then you may want to make arrangements for your post to be forwarded. Get organised about paying your bills online and make sure your health insurance will cover you wherever you are.

Sail Off into the Sunset

Twenty years from now you will be more disappointed by the things that you didn't do than by the ones you did do. So throw off the bowlines. Sail away from the safe harbour. Catch the trade winds in your sails. Explore. Dream. Discover.

MARK TWAIN

Sailing isn't the cheapest hobby but, like many dreams, it's affordable if you're prepared to make sacrifices elsewhere and as long as you don't feel the need to own a swanky gin palace. If you own your home, it's possible you could downsize in order to rent or own a modest sailboat and see some beautiful places. You could offset some costs by renting out your home for the months you're away.

Those who have managed to do it themselves recommend that if you don't have a lot of money to invest but would love to fulfil the dream, then sign up for a course of lessons, read everything you can about sailing adventures, and don't give up. Jan Irons met her husband David while on a sailing course and, now that they are retired, they spend six months a year in the sunny Caribbean, living cheaply like locals and eating fish they catch themselves. 'My husband had one rule: Whatever we did when we retired, it had to be done in shorts.'

For a budget alternative that still allows you to wear a funny hat and shout 'ahoy there!' at strangers, how about renting a narrowboat or cruising boat for a week on a river in the UK?

> ### *Do Something Really Different for a Year*
>
> *Remember how quickly your birthday used to roll around again when you were on the treadmill of work? It didn't seem possible that twelve months had passed, yet within that time you could have the adventure of your life.*

A Place in the Sun

Those who find growing old terrible are people who haven't done what they wanted with their lives.

MARTHA GELLHORN, WRITER

For years you've had to live in a particular place because of your job. Now – you're free to choose. If you're not necessarily tied to the place you currently live, perhaps it's time to think about a change. If you find a place you love, the chances are your friends and family will relish coming to visit.

Perhaps you'd prefer to live by the sea or surrounded by mountains, so you can indulge your passion for outdoor activities easily? Would you like a place in the country where you can grow your own vegetables and explore natural landscapes, or a bijou pad right in the heart of a city with access to more cultural activities and events?

If you feel you'd be happy in another country and there's nothing to hold you back from going somewhere exotic, you can actually reduce your living costs by moving to a country that's cheaper and warmer. Downsize if you need to in order to move to your dream life – you might not need such a big house if you're spending more time at the beach… A new life might even inspire you to start a new part-time business, or write about your experiences. There is nothing to stop you from going to live in a foreign country for a while, and everything to be gained from the experience of a different culture.

Try Before You Buy

It's not always advisable to sell up unless you've done your research – you don't want to lose all your savings if things go wrong, after all. So renting a place can be a good way to find out whether your dream move is actually the right move.

Ten Books to Inspire You

Getting away from it all isn't always possible, but if you have a spare room, conservatory or shed, how about converting it into a library so you can escape with your imagination? Here are some inspiring books to take with you…

Chickens, Mules and Two Old Fools – Victoria Twead's hilarious story of moving to a Spanish village with her partner Joe.

Eat, Walk, Write: An American Senior's Year of Adventure in Paris and Tuscany – Boyd Lemon retires from law aged 69 and moves to Europe for a fulfilling year.

Narrow Dog to Carcassonne – Terry Darlington and his wife, on retirement, decided to sail a narrowboat across the Channel and down through France to the Mediterranean.

Greece on My Wheels – Edward Enfield, recently retired and fuelled by a love of all things Greek, cycles rugged paths contemplating Byron, Lear and Classical history.

Dog Days in the Fortunate Islands: A New Life in Hidden Tenerife – John Searancke and his wife retire to the quiet north of Tenerife, learn Spanish and explore local cuisine.

The Olive Farm – Carol Drinkwater's adventures with a Provençal olive farm which she and her partner set about restoring.

Walking the Camino – Tony Kevin describes himself as an 'overweight, sedentary, 63-year-old former diplomat' as he sets off with just a backpack on a gruelling eight-week trek to Santiago de Compostela.

Britain from the Rails – Benedict le Vay finds a magical romance in train travel, and this is a leisurely sojourn around scenic routes and railway anecdotes.

Walking the County High Points of England – David Bathurst's ramble around the English counties conveys his love of the countryside in a light-hearted style.

Mud, Sweat and Gears – Ellie Bennett and her friend cycle from Land's End to John o' Groats via towpaths and back roads, sampling real ale along the way.

Explorer Events

 If you feel like taking off on a true adventure, attending talks by explorers who've done something extraordinary (and lived to tell the tale!) can be a great way of firing up your imagination, bolstering your courage and reminding you of important planning details. It can also be a way of meeting others in the audience – there's usually an opportunity to mingle afterwards – who may have done something similar. You could even find a companion for your trip. The Royal Geographical Society is an obvious place to start in London, but an increasing number of smaller groups organise low-key events, including Night of Adventure and Globetrotters – both with hubs around the UK.

FINDING FULFILMENT

Retirement is the last opportunity for individuals to reinvent themselves, let go of the past, and find peace and happiness within.

ERNIE ZELINSKI, WRITER

You've left behind one kind of stress – the deadlines, the commuting – but don't be surprised if another type starts to nag away at you. Retirement may come as a shock to the system, a culture shock. If you're the type of person who lives their job 24/7, who lives *for* their work, and doesn't have friends that aren't colleagues or business associates, then you may experience an identity crisis if you don't have other interests and social circles to keep you satisfied.

But look at it positively – the greater the life-change, the more rewarding it can be. An emotional upheaval might end up as an opportunity to get to know yourself better and find what you really want: whether it's spending more time with family and friends, or fulfilling your potential in any number of other areas. This is when you get to discover the new you.

You have plenty of time to master this, so don't be hard on yourself and think everyone else is doing better than you are. If you've been busy right up to retirement, it's going to take a while to figure things out from here.

Something Missing

Some people know exactly what they're going to do when they retire. For others, it can be more of a challenge once the initial fuss is over and everyone else is getting on with their lives without asking what you're doing with yours. Especially if you've retired before your friends, you may need a sense of purpose and something to give you a feeling of accomplishment at the end of the day – and something to talk to your friends or partner about.

It's natural, once the adrenalin rush of freedom wears off, to have difficulties adjusting to being less in demand and having less authority and power. How can the old place function without you? Even if you're proud of the legacy you've left behind in your old workplace, it can be hard to accustom yourself to the lack of urgent challenges in your day. This affects freelance workers just as much as it affects the newly retired. You're not alone. But what are you going to do about it?

Defining Yourself

Finding a new way to define yourself – instead of by a job title – is going to be important. When you're introduced to someone and aren't sure what you 'do' any more, just find a light-hearted way to fill the awkward space in the conversation until you figure it out. You could always try responding, 'Whatever I want!'

You may also need something to 'belong' to. Clubs, societies, classes and giving something back to the community will all give you something to talk about when you describe who you are. A volunteering commitment can also give you a routine, a place you need to be, if you find life in retirement too lacking in structure. If you require discipline to ensure you get outdoors and meet people, then a new part-time role could be just what you need, and help you to enjoy your leisure time more.

Personal Growth and Psychological Health

Professor Carol Ryff is Director of the Institute on Aging at the University of Wisconsin-Madison, and during a study of health and well-being she pinpointed six components of psychological health:

Self-acceptance – accepting yourself as you are, with all your strengths and weaknesses.

Positive relatedness – caring for and identifying with others.

Autonomy – living your own life, rather than following the dictates of others.

Environmental mastery – creating surroundings that suit your personal needs and capacities.

Personal growth – continuing to develop your personal potential through learning and experience.

Purpose in life – continuing to be creative and productive.

She noted that education increased the potential for personal growth and purpose in life. A sense of purpose is often achieved by charity work or active involvement in an organisation aligned with our personal beliefs that can make a difference in the world.

Community Projects – Men's Sheds

Men often find themselves isolated and alone when they retire from work, and while women traditionally find it easier to get involved in charity work informally, or join groups such as the Women's Institute, there have been fewer group activities especially for men.

So instead of retreating to your own shed in the garden, consider the phenomenon called Men's Sheds. Originating in Australia, it soon spread to other countries, providing a meeting place where men can find projects to work on together, making the most of their technical skills and experience. At a Men's Shed in Antrim, Northern Ireland, for example, the men have opened a charity shop to raise the funds to build, equip and staff two schools in a poverty-stricken area of Ethiopia. Their next project may involve restoring old engines.

The Shed is a place for ideas to brew, as well as a sense of belonging to something worthwhile. If there isn't one in your area, perhaps you should think about starting one with a few friends, or placing a local ad for others who might like to join.

Growing Better

In Norway, an academic study explored how those suffering from depression responded to the distraction of being involved in a horticultural programme. Author Marianne Thorsen Gonzalez found that those with moderate to severe symptoms improved after three months.

Volunteering

In Britain, over 50 per cent of volunteers are aged over 60. Volunteering in your community provides a valuable service to those in need, and can simultaneously increase your own well-being. The skills you've acquired during your working life could be much in demand in certain fields or could allow you to tutor at a community college. Volunteering keeps you active and in demand; interaction with others and the various other requirements of the role will help to keep you healthy.

Most towns will have a centre of some kind that matches up volunteers with needy causes. Online sites such as www.do-it.org.uk in the UK, www.allforgood.org in the US and www.govolunteer.com.au in Australia, or international sites such as www.globalvolunteernetwork.org and www.volunteermatch.org, can be helpful in finding specific roles or simply ideas about what might be out there. If you don't think your skills are so easily transferable or would like to do something completely different for a change, opportunities might include:

- Hospitals – hospices and large hospitals are always in need of volunteers to help with patients and family support
- Charity shop assistant
- Visitor guide at an art gallery or museum, or perhaps at your favourite natural heritage site
- Maintenance or gardening
- Working with the Samaritans
- Providing meals on wheels
- Administrative, marketing or lobbying work for a cause you believe in
- Animal rescue – feeding and exercising the animals
- Working with children with special needs
- Befriending the elderly, either in an official capacity or simply in your neighbourhood
- Homeless shelter assistance
- First aid training or other health outreach
- Sports events, such as directing crowds and handing water to participants at marathons

Live Your Own Life

The new experiences just waiting to happen are endless. Live your retirement to the full, but most of all, live it the way you want to live it. As Steve Jobs said, 'Your time is limited, so don't waste it living someone else's life.' You can now choose how you spend your days, and with whom – things and people that make you happy and fulfilled.

Teaching and Mentoring

Why waste all that knowledge and experience – why not pass it along to the younger generation through teaching, mentoring or coaching? It can give you a sense of achievement with every single session. Volunteer teachers are much in demand in developing countries, and practical skills can be particularly useful, especially in the health field. The VSO (Voluntary Service Overseas) organisation is respected for its high-quality programmes.

If you've worked in business, then perhaps a start-up entrepreneur would value your mentorship. Imagine the satisfaction of seeing a business flourish thanks to your advice. Young entrepreneurs may have the ideas and energy, but the odds of turning their passion into something sustainable increase with the guidance of an experienced professional willing to look over their business plan, pass on knowledge and help solve problems.

Sports Coaching

 If you're involved in a sports club but don't feel up to playing every week any more, you may find coaching the most useful role you've ever played. Rugby enthusiast Steven Gauge writes, 'Rugby retains a loyal family... ready to pick up a tackle bag and coach and support the next generation of players.' You'll still be part of the club, but without the injuries. According to Sport England, many clubs simply would not be able to function without volunteers and coaches, and they therefore 'play a vital role in community sport... In short, volunteers and coaches make sport happen.' Sport England therefore helps the volunteers through training programmes.

Try and Try Again

Don't leave it too long to discover your passions. Try out a variety of hobbies. Maybe the activity you'd always thought you wanted to pursue in retirement won't fulfil you at all, but you'll find something else by chance. The things you get involved with now will shape the next years of your life and determine your future happiness.

Raising Money for Charity

By the age of retirement, most of us have a cause of choice we'd like to do more about – the planet itself and its endangered species, poverty in a particular country, or research for a disease. So do something about it in a bigger way by raising awareness and money. Here are some ideas of ways to raise money and make an impact:

- Sponsored aerobics-a-thon

- Open day of gardens in your area

- Donate a percentage of sales of your book/paintings/tickets for a show

- Fundraising bad poetry night

- Sell your garden produce and jams

- Sponsored 100-mile (160-km) bike ride

- Organise a live music and dance night and sell tickets

- Fundraising football tournament

- Get your friends to create decadent cakes for an auction night

Meditation

Arianna Huffington, author and creator of the hugely successful online newspaper *The Huffington Post*, recommends meditating every day. After experiencing a crisis in her life due to sleep deprivation, she started to spend some time meditating every day and to make a point of including 'wisdom, wonder and giving' into her life. It was a turning point for her. So perhaps you should consider it at this turning point in yours.

Meditation is a broad term but in all its manifestations it's a form of training the mind, sometimes just by sitting still and closing your eyes in order to clear away negative thoughts. It's been practised since antiquity, and Buddhist monks meditate during their daily activities, focusing on awareness of the given task rather than being distracted by the past or future – a practice which is increasingly referred to as mindfulness or living in the moment.

Many meditate to achieve a calmer state of mind, but you can also incorporate a mantra – a repeated word or phrase – into your meditation to focus yourself on a goal such as positive thinking, patience or compassion.

Plan Your Year

If you're used to working towards goals, then be your own boss, and set targets for yourself for the year. Give yourself an appraisal at the end of the year: have you achieved what you set out to do? Perhaps you'll be ready to take on more responsibility next year – or maybe you'll want to reduce your hours. Think about whether you're happy in your new life-role.

CHAPTER 10

EXTREME THINGS
TO DO IN RETIREMENT

Be eccentric now. Don't wait for old age to wear purple.
REGINA BRETT, WRITER AND INSPIRATIONAL SPEAKER

You are only young once, but you can be immature for a lifetime.
JOHN P. GRIER, WRITER

So what else is left? You've gone through all the joys of retirement but you still feel you should do something just a little bit silly before it's too late? Campanology wasn't eccentric enough? If you take up any of the following, at least you'll never be stuck for dinner party conversation.

Photograph as many species
of wildlife as possible

Brew your own beer

Make people think

Start a nostalgia film club

Get to grips with philosophy

Get a job in a coffee shop to gather
material for your novel

Climb a very high mountain
(and stay there overnight)

Go into politics
(not the best way to
make friends, though)

Learn to play a concerto

Translate a book

MEDIUM SUBLIME

VERY SUBLIME

Become a cheesemaker

Open a jazz club

Become a film extra (especially good as most parts are nonspeaking, so you don't have to memorise lines; www.extras.com)

Go on a bike ride with your friend or partner on a bicycle made for two

Start a novelty tea cosy collection

MEDIUM RIDICULOUS

VERY RIDICULOUS

Swim with sharks

Video a dance routine with a group of friends and upload it onto YouTube

Get a tattoo

Take up rock climbing

Start a silly hat movement

Pursue Your Childhood Dream

When she was young, growing up in Los Angeles, Andrea Peterson was rescued from a burning building by firefighters, and on being saved she told them she wanted to be one of them when she grew up. They laughed, saying she could be a good mother, maybe even a teacher or a nurse, but never a fireman. After a strict upbringing, she left behind her childhood dream and had various other jobs, including medical transcriptionist and professional ballerina – until she was 61, living in Vermont, when she read a newspaper article about riding in the town's ambulance to observe what they do. It sparked something inside her.

A neighbour who worked in the fire department allowed her to accompany him on duty one day, and they had an ambulance call; she found the situation rewarding and fulfilling, and started taking courses, wishing she'd done it earlier. At first the young guys on the firefighting course couldn't accept her. But at 66, Andrea Peterson received her certification and became a firefighter. 'I had to wait a lifetime to be the real me,' she wrote.

Invent Something

 Peter Mark Roget was born in 1779 in England, son of a minister of the French Protestant Church, his family descended from Swiss ancestors. His career as a medical doctor kept him busy, but in his spare time during his early working years, he started classifying and cataloguing words according to their meaning. He had to put it aside eventually because of the demands of work, but after retirement at the age of 61, he spent the next few years on what would finally be published in 1852 – and after being revised many times, is still in print today – known simply as 'the thesaurus'. Quite a legacy he achieved in his retirement.

*Wacky Races**

Each year, thousands of people participate in extreme marathons, bicycle rides, triathlons and other endurance tests. They pit themselves against the elements in the most remote locations and take on the world's toughest challenges. This could be you.

Seriously, you're reading on? OK…

Of Scotland's 283 Munros (mountains higher than 3,000 feet or 914 metres), Sgurr Dearg on the Isle of Skye is known as the Inaccessible Pinnacle, requiring a 164-foot (50-metre) vertical rock climb.

Every June, triathletes meet to undertake the Escape from Alcatraz – a gruelling swim–cycle–run event from the infamous maximum-security prison to San Francisco.

From Eagle Plains, Yukon Territory to Tuktoyaktuk, Northwest Territories on the banks of the Arctic Ocean, the 6633 Ultra race is an extreme ultramarathon over 350 miles (563 km) with all your kit personally carried or pulled by sled. There is a shorter version of 'only' 120 miles (193 km) if you're not that fit.

And There's More...

The Everest Marathon starts near Base Camp and follows 26.2 miles (42.16 km) over rough but spectacular mountain trails in the world's highest marathon every two years.

The Jungle Marathon is held in Brazil each October: choose between 63 miles (101 km) or 150 miles (240 km) of ultimate eco-race with 40-degree temperatures, swamps and river crossings, dense jungle canopy, 99-per-cent humidity and the possibility of meeting a caiman, piranha or anaconda.

The Legendary Ultimate Challenge MudRun in Columbia, South Carolina, was designed and built by a former Marine drill instructor, with military-style obstacles day and night; they say 'you will sweat, you will probably bleed, and yes, you might break some bones'.

What – you're thinking of collecting tea cosies instead?

* We're not actually *recommending* you do any of these, unless you're a retired super-athlete aged 25.

Take Ballet Lessons

 John Lowe, a grandfather and former prisoner of war in World War Two, started taking ballet lessons at the age of 79 and performed into his nineties with the Lantern Dance Company in Cambridgeshire, England. 'Dancing is the most amazing feeling,' he says. 'It is a joy to move to beautiful music.' A former theatre manager and art teacher and a whizz at DIY, he built himself a trapeze at home, laid a wooden floor and installed a ballet bar. At the time of writing, he still takes ballet classes, aged 94.

Start a World-famous Franchise

'Colonel' Harland Sanders, born in Indiana in 1890, started cooking for his family from the age of six after his father died and his mother had to go out to work. After doing a series of other jobs, at the age of 40 he was running a service station in Kentucky when he began cooking for hungry travellers, and eventually set up a restaurant across the street. He was at the age of retirement, 65, when a new highway directed traffic away from his business, so he set about developing a franchise for his chicken recipe. Less than a decade later, there were 600 outlets of Kentucky Fried Chicken and he sold his interest in the company for $2 million. He went on to live to the grand old age of 90.

Go for It, Grandpa/Grandma...

I hope the record inspires others to realise it's never too late.

JOHANNA QUAAS, ON BEING INCLUDED IN THE
GUINNESS WORLD RECORDS AS THE WORLD'S OLDEST GYMNAST

Feel a little bit past it? Simon Gandolfi from England, author of *Old Man on a Bike* and *Old Men Can't Wait*, spent his seventies travelling alone by motorcycle around India and the Americas. Helmut Wirz from Germany, a former pharmacist, became the world's oldest bungee-jumper at the age of 87. In 2013 Englishman Paul Freedman was officially the oldest runner in the London Marathon at 88; he didn't start running marathons until he was 61. That same year Johanna Quaas, a German retired PE teacher, was recorded as the world's oldest gymnast at 86. Some call it 'ageing with attitude'.

Canadians Don and Alison were aged 68 and 61 respectively when they decided to sell their home in order to travel the world and live a nomadic life. Don's career as a neuropsychologist had been stressing him to the point of sickness. Two years later they were swimming with elephants and climbing volcanoes. 'He's so much healthier and happier than when he was working,' said Alison in an interview with blogger Nomadic Matt.

When American Lew Hollander completed an Ironman triathlon in October 2012 at the age of 82, he held the record as the world's oldest Ironman champion. An Ironman comprises a 2.4-mile (3.9-km) swim, a 112-mile (180-km) bike ride and a marathon run, without a break. His arch-rival is fellow American Sister Madonna Buder, aka the Iron Nun, who holds the record as the oldest woman ever to complete an Ironman triathlon, also at the age of 82. The Roman Catholic nun was inducted into the USA Triathlon Hall of Fame in Chicago aged 84. 'If you don't think age and you just get up and do and you think you're a teenager, well, you'll start to act like one,' she said.

Lew's Secret: The Pizza Diet

By this, Ironman Lew Hollander doesn't mean just eating pizza. But just as a pizza includes a variety of ingredients, he reckons you should eat a variety of different foods from different places, collecting a wide spectrum of nutrients. He especially recommends kelp, and avoiding all processed foods; and he extols the benefits of a good, stable relationship and staying involved both physically and mentally.

EPILOGUE

I love everything that's old: old friends, old times, old manners, old books, old wine.

OLIVER GOLDSMITH, WRITER AND POET

If you've already retired, start thinking about the year to come. What's the one biggest thing you'd like to achieve between now and this time next year? Write it down, with as many details as you can think of. Use this as a motivator to set you on the right path. Then write down three other things you'd like to start doing. It will be interesting to look back next year and see if you've met, changed or surpassed your goals.

If you're reading this book before retirement, bravo! You've got plenty of time to plan ahead.

CONGRATULATIONS
— ON YOUR —
RETIREMENT

TED HEYBRIDGE

CONGRATULATIONS ON YOUR RETIREMENT

Ted Heybridge

ISBN: 978 1 84953 624 0   Hardback   £5.99

Say hello to stress-free lie-ins and relaxing afternoon strolls, to having all the time in the world to do what YOU want to do! This delightful little book will help you through retirement with a smile on your face.

If you're interested in finding out more about our books,
find us on Facebook at **Summersdale Publishers**
and follow us on Twitter at **@Summersdale**.

www.summersdale.com